Praying with
Ignatius of Loyola

12 hrs No food after 4pm
2 hrs Water til 6 am

**Other Books by Jacqueline Syrup Bergan
and Marie Schwan, CSJ**

Love

Forgiveness

Other Books and Resources on Ignatian Spirituality

What Is Ignatian Spirituality?

A Friendship Like No Other

A Simple, Life-Changing Prayer

God Finds Us

An Ignatian Book of Days

www.IgnatianSpirituality.com

Praying with
Ignatius of Loyola

Jacqueline Bergan
Marie Schwan, CSJ

Chicago

LOYOLA PRESS.
A JESUIT MINISTRY

3441 N. Ashland Avenue
Chicago, Illinois 60657
(800) 621-1008
www.loyolapress.com

Cover art credit: Sue Kouma Johnson

ISBN-13: 978-0-8294-4352-3
ISBN-10: 0-8294-4352-5
Library of Congress Control Number: 2015935394

Printed in the United States of America.

15 16 17 18 19 20 Versa 10 9 8 7 6 5 4 3 2 1

To our Jesuit friends and brothers in Christ

Contents

Foreword

Companions for the Journey

Just as food is required for human life, so are companions. Indeed, the word *companions* comes from two Latin words: *com*, meaning "with," and *panis*, meaning "bread." Companions nourish our heart, mind, soul, and body. They are also the people with whom we can celebrate the sharing of bread.

Perhaps the most touching stories in the Bible are about companionship: the Last Supper, the wedding feast at Cana, the sharing of the loaves and the fishes, and Jesus' breaking of bread with the disciples he met on the road to Emmaus. Each incident of companionship with Jesus revealed more about his mercy, love, wisdom, suffering, and hope. When Jesus went to pray in the Garden of Olives, he craved the companionship of the apostles. They let him down. But God sent the Spirit to inflame the hearts of the apostles, and they became faithful companions to Jesus and to one another.

Throughout history, other faithful companions have followed Jesus and the apostles. These saints and mystics have made the journey from conversion, through suffering, to resurrection. Just as they were inspired by the holy people who went before them, so may you enjoy the companionship of the saints as you make your spiritual journey. One such good companion is St. Ignatius of Loyola.

The spiritual hunger that has become so evident over the past few decades—through social media, new websites, and endless new books—is a great sign of renewal in Christian life. People fill retreat programs and workshops on topics in spirituality. The demand for spiritual directors exceeds the number available. Interest in the life and writings of saints and mystics is increasing as people search for models of whole and holy Christian life.

Praying with Ignatius

Praying with Ignatius of Loyola is more than just a book about Ignatius's spirituality. This book seeks to engage you in praying as Ignatius did about issues and themes that were central to his experience. Each meditation can enlighten your understanding of his spirituality and lead you to reflect on your own experience.

The goal of *Praying with Ignatius of Loyola* is that you will discover Ignatius's profound spirituality and integrate his spirit and wisdom into your relationship with God, with your brothers and sisters, and with your own heart and mind.

Suggestions for Praying with Ignatius

Meet Ignatius of Loyola, a courageous and fascinating companion for your pilgrimage, by reading the introduction to this book. It provides a brief biography of Ignatius and an outline of the major themes of his spirituality.

Once you meet Ignatius, you will be ready to pray with him and to encounter God, your sisters and brothers, and yourself in new and wonderful ways. To help your prayer, here are some suggestions rooted in the tradition of Christian spirituality.

Create a sacred space. Jesus said, "But whenever you pray, go into your room and shut the door and pray to your [God] who is in secret; and your [God] who sees in secret will reward you" (Matthew 6:6). Solitary prayer is best done in a place where you can have privacy and silence, both of which can be luxuries for busy people. If privacy and silence are not possible, create a quiet, safe place within yourself, perhaps while riding to and from work, while sitting at the dentist's office, or while waiting for someone. Do the best you can, knowing that our loving God is present everywhere. Whether the meditations in this book are used for solitary prayer or with a group, try to create a prayerful mood with candles, meditative music, an open Bible, or a crucifix.

Open yourself to the power of prayer. Every human experience has a religious dimension. All of life is suffused with God's presence. So remind yourself that God is present as you begin your period of prayer. Do not worry about distractions. If something keeps intruding during your prayer, spend some time talking with God about it. Be flexible, because God's Spirit blows where it will.

Prayer can open your mind and widen your vision. Be open to new ways of seeing God, people, and yourself. As you open yourself to the Spirit of God, different emotions might be evoked, such as sadness from tender memories or joy from a celebration recalled. Our emotions are messages from God that can tell us much about our spiritual quest. Also, prayer strengthens our will to act. Through prayer, God can touch our will and empower us to live according to what we know is true.

Finally, many of the meditations in this book will call you to employ your memories, your imagination, and the circumstances of your life as subjects for prayer. The great mystics and saints realized that they had to use all their resources to know God better. Indeed, God speaks to us continually and touches us constantly. We must learn to listen and feel with all the means that God has given us.

Come to prayer with an open mind, heart, and will.

Preview each meditation before beginning. After you have placed yourself in God's presence, spend a few moments previewing the readings and especially the reflection activities. Several reflection activities are given in each meditation because different styles of prayer appeal to different personalities or personal needs. Note that each meditation has more reflection activities than can be done during one prayer period. Therefore, select only one or two reflection activities each time you use a meditation. Do not feel compelled to complete all the reflection activities.

Read meditatively. Each meditation presents a story about Ignatius and a reading from his writings. Take your time reading. If a particular phrase touches you, stay with it. Relish its feelings, meanings, and concerns.

Use the reflections. Following the readings is a short reflection in commentary form, which is meant to give perspective to the readings. Then you are offered several ways of meditating on the readings and the theme of the prayer. You may be familiar with the different methods of meditating, but in case you are not, they are described briefly here:

- *Repeated short prayer:* One means of focusing your prayer is to repeat a single word or a short phrase taken from the readings or from the Scriptures. For example, a phrase to use in a meditation on surrendering to God's will might be "Take me, Lord!" Repeated slowly and in harmony with your breathing, the prayer helps you center your heart and mind on one action or attribute of God.

- *Lectio divina:* This type of meditation is "divine studying," a concentrated reflection on the word of God or the wisdom of a spiritual writer. Most often in *lectio divina*, you will be invited to read one of the passages several times and then concentrate on one or two sentences, pondering their meaning for you and their effect on you. *Lectio divina* commonly ends with formulation of a resolution.

- *Guided meditation:* In this type of meditation, our imagination helps us consider alternative actions and likely consequences. Our imagination helps us experience new ways of seeing God, our neighbors, ourselves, and nature. When Jesus told his followers parables and stories, he engaged their imaginations. In this book, you will be invited to follow guided meditations. One way of doing a guided meditation is to read the scene or story several times, until you know the outline and can recall it when you enter into reflection. Or before your prayer time, you may wish to record the meditation to play back. If so, remember to allow pauses for reflection between phrases and to speak with a slow, peaceful pace and tone. Then, during prayer, when you have finished the readings and the reflection commentary, you can turn on your recording of the meditation and be led through it. If you find your own voice too distracting, ask a friend to make the recording for you.

- *Examen of consciousness*: The reflections often will ask you to examine how God has been speaking to you in your past and present experience—in other words, the reflections will ask you to examine your awareness of God's presence in your life.

- *Journal writing*: Writing is a process of discovery. If you write for any length of time, stating honestly what is on your mind and in your heart, you will unearth much about who you are, how you stand with God, the deep longings that reside in your soul, and more. In some reflections, you will be asked to write a dialogue with Jesus or someone else. If you have never used writing as a means of meditation, try it. Reserve a special notebook for your journal writing. If you'd like, you can go back to your entries at a future time for an examen of consciousness.

- *Action*: Occasionally, a reflection will suggest singing a favorite hymn, going out for a walk, or undertaking some other physical activity. Actions can be meaningful forms of prayer.

Using the Meditations for Group Prayer

If you wish to use the meditations for community prayer, these suggestions may help:

- Read the theme to the group. Call the community into the presence of God, using the short opening prayer. Invite one or two participants to read one or both readings. If you use both readings, observe the pause between them.

- The reflection commentary may be used as a reading, or it can be omitted, depending on the needs and interests of the group.

- Select one of the reflection activities for your group. Allow sufficient time for your group to reflect, to recite a centering prayer, to accomplish a studying prayer (*lectio divina*), or to finish an examen of consciousness. Depending on the group and the time available, you may want to invite the participants to share their reflections, responses, or petitions with the group.

- Reading the passage from Scripture may serve as a summary of the meditation.

- If a formulated prayer or a psalm is given as a closing, it may be recited by the entire group. Or you may ask participants to offer their own prayers for the closing.

Now you are ready to begin praying with Ignatius of Loyola, a faithful and caring companion on this stage of your spiritual journey. Over the past five centuries, Ignatius has drawn countless people to seek a closer relationship with God. We hope that you will find him to be a true soul companion.

Introduction

As July 31, 1556, was dawning, Ignatius of Loyola uttered his last words, "O my God!" Quickly, the news of his death spread through the streets of Rome. People exclaimed, "The saint has died."

In 1622, Ignatius was indeed proclaimed a saint. Pope Gregory XIII's declaration echoed what people knew all along: "Ignatius had a heart big enough to hold the universe" (Purcell, *The First Jesuit: Saint Ignatius Loyola*, iv). Certainly Ignatius had founded a new religious community, schools and universities, and institutions to serve those living in poverty, but people most remembered his great and generous heart, which embraced women and men of all kinds and the God who dwelled among them.

Even though Ignatius lived five hundred years ago, his spirituality remains a rock of strength and wisdom. His Spiritual Exercises continue to guide men and women to a more profound commitment to Christ. His story exemplifies unabashed love for God and courageous love for other people. Ignatius challenges us to follow him in doing all things for the greater glory of God.

Ignatius's Story

The words *revolution* and *discovery* describe the world into which Ignatius was born in 1491. Within a year of his birth, the monarchs Ferdinand V of Castile and his wife, Isabella I, had thrown off the yoke of Moorish rule in Spain by their victory at Granada. In conquering their Islamic overlords, they soon imposed harsh terms on the vanquished: Moors had to choose among baptism, emigration, and severe punishment. Not satisfied with these measures, the Crown instituted the Inquisition to root out heresy among converted Jews, Moors, and suspect Christians. Religious orthodoxy became a test of loyalty to the Spanish monarchy and a way to bring people into line.

Twenty-five years after the unification of Spain and the birth of Ignatius, another revolution rocked Europe: the Protestant Reformation. In 1517 Martin Luther unrolled a large poster and fastened it to the door of Wittenberg Cathedral. The ninety-five theses on that poster kindled the fires of reform that had been smoldering for years. John Calvin, another contemporary of Ignatius's and also a graduate of the University of Paris, would take the Reformation in radical new directions. And in England, Henry VIII divorced his country from Roman Catholicism.

While these revolutions shattered church unity and sundered nations, new lands were being claimed, explored, and exploited by European powers. The Portuguese sailed around the southern tip of Africa in 1486. Then in 1492, Christopher Columbus walked on the shores of the New World. These discoveries spurred a furious competition among the countries of Europe to expand their spheres of influence and national treasuries. Dutch, Spanish, Portuguese, and English ships sailed the high seas, hoping to bring home fame and fortune. For the church, each new land claimed by a Catholic country was also claimed for by Catholicism.

The Reformation and the "new" worlds in which to proclaim the reign of God would prove to be major influences on Ignatius and on his companions of the Society of Jesus.

Ignatius's Youth

Iñigo López de Oñaz y Loyola was born in the castle of Loyola near the small town of Azpeitia in the Basque province of Guipúzcoa,

Spain. The Loyolas had loyally served the Crown and had been rewarded generously. Iñigo's father, Beltrán, led troops against the Moors. His older brother Juan Pérez died in Spain's capture of the Kingdom of Naples. Another brother, Hernando, was killed in royal service in the New World.

Iñigo (he started calling himself Ignatius while studying in Paris) was the youngest child in a family of seven sons and four daughters. Marina Saenz de Lieona y Balda, his mother, died when he was very young. His care was entrusted to a wet nurse, María Garín, a woman from a nearby farm. As a child of seven, Iñigo returned to the family home, then under the direction of his brother Martín García, heir to the family estate. Martín's bride, Madalena de Aroaz—devout, cultured, and formerly a lady-in-waiting to Queen Isabella—became the mother Iñigo had lost. Little more is known of Iñigo's childhood. Perhaps few people expected much of this youngest son of Beltrán of Loyola.

Young Manhood

Evidently Iñigo's father intended that the boy would become a priest. As a child, Iñigo was tonsured—that is, he had a patch of hair clipped from the top of his head as a sign of his dedication to clerical formation. Giving the youngest son to the church was common at the time. But by the time Iñigo was an adolescent, the incompatibility of his character and the clerical life had become apparent. Indeed, Iñigo wore his blond hair at shoulder length and went about in bright garb, including a red cap with a waving feather. The only time he alluded to his tonsure was during litigation against him. Having been tonsured, Iñigo claimed that he should be tried in ecclesiastical court instead of the harsher civil court.

During his early teens, Iñigo left the family house and rode to the town of Arévalo to serve as a page in the house of the royal treasurer Juan Velázquez de Cuéllar, a relative and friend of the Loyola family. In this household, Iñigo began to prepare for the career of a courtier and soldier.

The elegant courts to which he rode at the side of his new master stirred all the latent gallantry of Iñigo's heart. He led the life of a young, single male courtier: he gambled, brawled, and fought duels. He flirted and dallied with women and became a special admirer of the Infanta Catarina, the youngest sister of Emperor Charles V.

When Queen Isabella died, Ferdinand married a fifteen-year-old Frenchwoman, Germana. After Ferdinand died, Velázquez found himself resisting the avaricious demands of the young widowed queen. She summarily dismissed and disgraced Velázquez. People abandoned him. His debts mounted, and a son died. In 1517, broken by so much adversity, Velázquez himself died, leaving Iñigo masterless and disillusioned.

Iñigo rode north, seeking a new lord to serve. He enlisted in the army of the viceroy of Navarre and soon found himself defending Pamplona, the capital of Navarre, with a few hundred other soldiers against a besieging French army of twelve thousand. Iñigo persuaded the commander not to surrender without a fight. Encouraged by Iñigo's valor, the soldiers joined in the defense. On May 20, 1517, during the battle, a cannonball shattered Iñigo's right leg and badly injured the left.

After the fall of Pamplona, the French treated Iñigo's wounds and saw that he was carried back to his home in Loyola. The two-week trip through the mountains proved torturous. When Iñigo arrived home, doctors discovered that the bones of his right leg had been badly set. Even if the leg healed, it would be shorter, and a bone was protruding. Iñigo demanded that the bone be rebroken and set straight. He hovered near death many times in the weeks that followed. On the feast of St. Peter, to whom Iñigo had a special devotion, he began to improve.

Conversion

Having long hours on his hands during the recuperation, Iñigo asked to read the popular tales of romance and chivalry. None could be found in the castle, so he was given the lives of Christ and the saints to read. Gradually, Iñigo experienced an inner conversion. His external wounding was the occasion for his inner healing.

Whenever Iñigo fantasized about the glorious deeds he would do as a soldier, he felt momentarily happy. When the fantasies left him, he felt let down and discontented. In contrast, when he contemplated the great and holy deeds of the saints, especially Dominic and Francis of Assisi, he experienced exhilaration and energy. Iñigo realized that only doing God's will would lead him to true peace. From then on, the zeal that he had shown in soldiering and pursuing women was redirected to the service of the greater glory of God.

Iñigo's immediate concern was to repent and be cleansed of the sins of his youth. He decided to first go to the famous mountain monastery of Montserrat and make a thorough confession there and then do penance. From Montserrat he would make a pilgrimage to Jerusalem, where he hoped to stay and minister to other pilgrims and bring unbelievers to Christ.

Iñigo was thirty years old. The year was 1521. In Rome, St. Peter's Basilica was being built. The pope had excommunicated Martin Luther. John Calvin was eleven years old, and Teresa of Ávila, six. The church was about to elect Pope Adrian VI, a reformer. The European nations were vying for power in, and possession of, the New World. Into this milieu, the pilgrim Iñigo set out on his penitential journey.

Cleansing and Enlightenment at Montserrat and Manresa

Once at Montserrat, Iñigo stripped himself of his belongings, put on a beggar's garb, and made a general confession. He spent the night before the feast of Mary, on March 25, 1522, in a vigil of prayer. Having surrendered his dagger and sword as offerings to the Black Madonna of Montserrat, he then surrendered himself totally to God, the only ruler he would serve for the rest of his life.

Disarmed and vulnerable, Iñigo next made his way from Montserrat to the small village of Manresa, where he spent several months living at a Dominican monastery. He prayed, he fasted, he slept on a slab of stone. He experienced the ridicule of the street children, who jeered at the barefoot beggar he had become. His fervor to make reparation for his sins led him to extreme penitential practices. The once-fastidious Iñigo also visited and nursed patients in the local hospital, especially those with loathsome diseases.

During Iñigo's long vigils of prayer in caves around Manresa, the warm glow of peace that embraced him after his surrender to God at Montserrat was replaced by tormenting scruples. As the full scope of his sinfulness overwhelmed him, Iñigo almost despaired that God could ever forgive him. So distraught did he become that he once pleaded with God, "Show me, O Lord, where I may find it [release from scruples]; even though I should have to follow a little dog so he could help me, I would do it" (*The Autobiography of Saint Ignatius Loyola*, 35). His trial lifted only when he humbly obeyed his confessor, who ordered him to break a prolonged, self-inflicted fast. Gradually, he allowed the comfort of God's grace into his soul.

During Iñigo's time at Manresa, God also blessed him with deep and consoling spiritual experiences. In his autobiography, he described visions that heightened his awareness of the Trinity, of creation, and of Christ's humanity. On the banks of the river Cardoner, he experienced an infusion of wisdom so profound that it nourished him for the remainder of his life. Using the third person to refer to himself, he declared, "The eyes of his understanding began to be opened . . . this was with so great an enlightenment that everything seemed new to him" (*Autobiography*, 39).

Eventually, Iñigo left Manresa on his long-desired pilgrimage to Jerusalem. Because he had no money, title, or possessions, he begged for alms and food, dependent on God's generosity. And as he traveled, he continued to document his inner journey. He wrote of his struggle with the darkness of sin and his desire for power, pleasure, and possessions. He wrote of his own self-offering to Christ and the step-by-step process of contemplating the incarnation and Christ's public life, passion, and resurrection. These writings served as the foundation of what would become his Spiritual Exercises, which outline a process of prayer and meditation designed to draw a person to conversion to Christ and to a total love for God. The Spiritual Exercises are the ongoing inheritance of the creative, spiritual genius of Iñigo. Their formulation illustrates that gradually the mind and heart of Christ were forming the mind and heart of Iñigo.

Pilgrimage to the Holy Land and Return Home

Needing the pope's permission to visit the Holy Land, Iñigo slowly wound his way to Rome, where he obtained the approval for his pilgrimage. Eventually, having begged the necessary money for the trip, he boarded a Venetian vessel bound for Jerusalem.

After a voyage of nearly six weeks, Iñigo finally set foot in the Holy Land. Burning with excitement, he visited all the holy places, but after only three weeks, the authorities ordered him to leave. The local religious officials feared that Iñigo would, like some overeager pilgrims before him, be killed or captured and held for ransom. So Iñigo headed home to Spain, disappointed that he could not stay in the Holy Land and bring souls to Christ. Nevertheless, planted firmly in his heart was the conviction that his lifelong work should be the conversion of those who occupied the Holy Land, to which he fully intended to return.

During the long journey home, Iñigo was taken prisoner twice, once by the French and once by the Spanish, who were fighting each other in Italy. Eventually Iñigo arrived in Barcelona. By this time, he knew that if he was going to preach the word of God, he had to have more knowledge. His education as a boy had not gone beyond the rudiments of reading and writing. So Iñigo took lessons in Latin. At thirty-three years of age, Iñigo studied along with boys age twelve and younger. After two years, he knew enough Latin to enter the university in Alcalá, where he wanted to study philosophy.

Alcalá and Salamanca

In Alcalá, Iñigo lived in a poorhouse and then a hospital. His income came from begging and giving instructions in the Spiritual Exercises. But life was hard for him. After years away from any study, learning came slowly. In addition, as a result of the extremes of his earlier penances, his health had progressively deteriorated. He suffered from fevers and digestive troubles that would plague him until he died. Perhaps most distressing to Iñigo were the periodic ecclesiastical inquiries into the orthodoxy of his informal preaching and his teaching of religion. At one point, the local church officials jailed him for forty-two days. Then they forbade him to teach or preach until he had completed his studies.

Convinced that God had called him to spread the good news, Iñigo and several companions who had joined him moved to Salamanca, where they thought they might be better received. Twelve days after arrival, Iñigo was jailed again, this time by a local community of Dominicans who suspected him of heresy. Although they cleared him of any charges, he was forbidden to preach freely.

In early 1528, realizing that he needed to finish his studies and make a new start, Iñigo set off for Paris.

Study in Paris

Iñigo began his study of philosophy at Montaigu College but soon ran out of money. On the advice of a friend, he undertook the first of three begging journeys to Flanders. These journeys provided sufficient funds for him to study undisturbed once back in Paris. By 1535, Iñigo—now called Ignatius, the Latinized version of the name *Iñigo*—had completed his studies in philosophy and theology, receiving the title "magister."

While studying, Ignatius had continued to teach the Spiritual Exercises. Drawn by his charism, fellow students were motivated to "make" the Spiritual Exercises and to adopt the ideals that inspired him. Among the first young men to accept the challenge presented by Ignatius were Peter Faber and Francis Xavier. As time passed, more men joined Ignatius, and the company grew in their attachment to Jesus.

Wanting to formalize their commitment, on August 15, 1534, Ignatius and six companions made vows of chastity and poverty and promised to make a pilgrimage to Jerusalem. Already the group had determined that if it was impossible to minister in Jerusalem, they would offer themselves in obedience to the pope, believing that he would know the places of greatest need to which they might go in service to the greater glory of God.

At this point, Ignatius's health failed him. His doctors and friends urged him to return to Spain to regain his strength. In the meantime, his companions would finish their theological studies and, by 1537, gather in Venice to embark on their pilgrimage to the Holy Land. Ignatius placed Peter Faber as head of the companions and rode south to his homeland. Arriving home, Ignatius did recover his health, despite continuing to preach, catechize, and give the Exercises.

Venice and the Road to Rome

At the end of 1535, Ignatius traveled from Spain to Venice. He delved into the study of theology, directed the Exercises, and waited for his companions to come from Paris. In January 1537, his companions arrived. While waiting for political changes that would allow their departure to Jerusalem, the companions ministered to people suffering from poverty and hunger, cared for the sick, and preached the gospel. On June 24, 1537, Ignatius was ordained to the priesthood, but he postponed his first Mass, hoping to offer it in the Holy Land.

Because of hostilities between the Venetians and the Ottomans, travel to the Holy Land ceased. The companions decided to go to Rome. By this time, they had begun to identify themselves as the Company of Jesus. During the journey to Rome, regretting that he could not fulfill his pledge to return to Jerusalem, Ignatius unburdened his heart and soul to God. Then he heard God say to him, "I will show you favor in Rome" (Rahner, *Ignatius of Loyola*, 58). With this assurance, Ignatius and his companions went forward in confidence.

The Society Takes Form

Once Ignatius and the company were in Rome, Pope Paul III urged them to undertake their ministry in the city. They continued to give the Spiritual Exercises. They taught religion, preached, and worked among Rome's poor population. During the bitter winter of 1538–39, famine stalked the city. Scores of people died of starvation or froze to death in the streets. The companions provided housing and food to those in need and devoted long hours to the sick and dying. Altogether they cared for more than three thousand people that winter. By then, Ignatius had realized that God meant for him to minister in Rome. So, in the face of so much misery, he offered his first Mass on Christmas Day at the Basilica of St. Mary Major.

The following spring, the companions began deliberations regarding their future. Should they stay together? Should they become a religious order? What should their ministry and organization be? As their discussions went forward, they became convinced that God had been calling them, partly because of the obvious fruits of their service thus far. On April 15, 1539, they unanimously decided to remain together, to structure their life in common, and to take a vow of obedience to one member who was to function as their leader. Almost immediately, Pope Paul III gave oral approval for founding the new religious order, the Society of Jesus. In 1540, the Catholic Church officially recognized the society. Despite his protests, Ignatius was elected its first general for life.

All for the Greater Glory of God

From his small office on Santa Maria della Strata, Ignatius administered and coordinated the activities of the expanding society. In response to requests from the pope, Ignatius sent Jesuits, as they were called—the most famous among them, Francis Xavier—to India and the Far East. He sent them to all parts of Europe, where they spearheaded the reformation and renewal of the church. Diego Laynez preached and taught in Italy and brilliantly represented the order at the Council of Trent. Peter Faber carried the good news on journeys from Portugal to Germany. Francis Borgia labored for Christ in Spain. The charism (spiritual gifts) and energy of Ignatius spread throughout the known world like "fire to the earth" (Luke 12:49).

Wherever members of the Society of Jesus went, they opened schools. In response to the needs of the time, education became a primary ministry. From parish to parish, Jesuit missionaries brought to the laity an inner renewal of faith through the Spiritual Exercises. At the same time, Jesuits continued to nurse the sick, feed the poor, and visit the imprisoned. Ignatius and the companions embraced the attitude of total availability, so that in all things the greater glory of God might be their first consideration.

While the companions served throughout the world, Ignatius labored in Rome. He spent much of his time writing letters to members of the society, giving them encouragement and direction. In addition to the duties incumbent upon him as general of the Society of Jesus, Ignatius guided people through the Spiritual Exercises, gave sermons, catechized, and established a residence for the rehabilitation of former prostitutes in Rome. He founded orphanages and a home for abandoned girls, who otherwise would easily be exploited.

Ignatius undertook another major task: writing, revising, and refining the constitutions of the society. Each day at Mass, he commended to God the particular point of the constitutions with which he was concerned. He then meditated on that point. The constitutions articulated the law of love that is the spirit and power of the Spiritual Exercises. When completed, they made concrete a pattern of life that formed a way to God.

Death in Rome

During his last years, Ignatius was tormented by a liver disease. Finally, on the evening of July 30, 1556, Ignatius asked his secretary to send for the papal blessing for the dying. In the middle of the night, a lay brother in the next room heard Ignatius pray, "O my God!" (*Ignatius of Loyola*, 62). In the early morning hours, Ignatius peacefully surrendered his life to God.

Upon his death, approximately one thousand companions carried on the mission of Ignatius. They went on to teach in forty-six colleges in Europe and ministered from 110 houses throughout the world.

Ignatius's Spirituality

Ignatius's spiritual legacy spread through the lives of his companions in the Society of Jesus. But he also left four important documents, as well as nearly seven thousand letters, that give shape and color to his spirituality. Dictated toward the end of his life, his autobiography tells the story of his conversion and life until 1538. His spiritual journal narrates a small part of his unfolding inner journey. Through his *Spiritual Exercises* and *Constitutions*, he systematically laid out guidelines for the spiritual life. From all these sources, the main threads of his spirituality can be outlined.

Encountering God in Our Experience

One unshakable belief Ignatius held was that God can be encountered in our experience. God comes directly to women and men, and they will recognize God's presence if they open their hearts and minds. The purpose of the Spiritual Exercises is to help people experience God directly and powerfully. When people encounter God, they are changed forever. Such an encounter frees people to love wholeheartedly.

For the Greater Glory of God

For Ignatius, to live meant to embrace the will of God generously and enthusiastically. To serve and glorify God became the compelling motive of his life.

Ignatius restlessly yearned for God. He experienced the thirst and emptiness that no power or possession could satiate. He longed for the total and consuming love that comes only from the source of all love. Once Ignatius felt the embrace of God's love, he strove with singleness of purpose for the greater glory of God.

The Spiritual Exercises urge retreatants to listen to the Holy
Spirit to discover God's will and what would serve the greater glory
of God. Through the process of his own conversion to life according to Christ, Ignatius learned a way of discernment that remains as
applicable today as it was five hundred years ago.

The Mysticism of Service

Ignatian spirituality does not demand withdrawal from the world.
Rather, Ignatius brought the word of God to classrooms and hospitals, orphanages and the halls of government. Wherever humans
suffered, the heart and hands of Ignatius followed with the compassion of Christ. No sacrifice was too great, no suffering too deep,
no poverty too excruciating, as long as the love of Christ would be
mediated in such a manner that those to whom he was ministering
would feel the tender compassion and comfort of Christ's presence.

While answering the call to serve individuals in need, Ignatius
sought to aid the reform of the church. He preached, taught, and
gave the Exercises, hoping to call the church through its leaders to
a rededication to God's reign.

The Call to Ongoing Conversion

Ignatius composed the Spiritual Exercises and the daily examen
of consciousness to help people answer the call to conversion to
Christ.

The Spiritual Exercises lead retreatants through a month-long
process that begins with a confrontation with their own sinfulness;
that continues with contemplation of the birth, public life, passion,
and resurrection of Jesus; and that concludes with meditations on
God's personal and unconditional love for each person. During
the Exercises, retreatants receive instructions about the three kinds
of humility, methods of prayer, and how to discern God's
will—among other topics. The retreat itself can be a powerful time

of turning toward God, and the methods of prayer and discernment are tools for the ongoing journey to God.

Devotion to the Church

For Ignatius, the church gave physical expression of the love that Jesus has for the people of God. The church served as a way to God and a symbol of God's mysterious love for humankind.

Ignatius's devotion to the church was motivated by his desire to serve the souls of Christians. Even though Ignatius saw the many human problems besetting the church in his time, his loyalty was unflinching. Although Ignatius was acutely aware of the probable ramifications presented by the difficulties in the church, he did not allow it to become a distraction. He made the deliberate choice to hold fast to his belief that the church remained a herald of God's word, a servant of God's people, a community of believers, and a sign of God's love.

Prayer That Permeates Daily Life

Ignatian spirituality invites people to daily prayer. In his writing, Ignatius described several methods of solitary prayer, and he encouraged people to develop the kind of prayer that best suits who they are and where they are on their spiritual journey. Ignatius recognized with great sensitivity that each individual has different gifts and a unique inner movement of soul. Ignatius approached prayer not only with his intellect, memory, and will but also with his senses and with active imagination.

The Discipline of the Ordinary

Contrary to the practices of his time, Ignatius encouraged moderation in fasting and penitence. He knew that meeting with love the ordinary frictions and trials of family, community, ministry, and the workplace required self-sacrifice and discipline enough to test anyone.

Ignatius also counseled adequate care of physical health. He appreciated the gift of food and recreation, acknowledging that health of mind and body were essential for one to be effective in ministry, seeking the greater glory of God.

Ignatius for Today

The desire for love, hope, and wholeness burns in the hearts of people today just as it burned in the heart of Ignatius. Ignatius's time had its demons, and so does ours. They may not really be so different.

The way to God that emerged from Ignatius's own conversion can still lead us to freedom from the demons of our age: addictions, greed, emptiness of heart, despair, confusion, violence, and meaninglessness. Through the centuries, the Spiritual Exercises, which are the heart of Ignatian spirituality, have been a powerful means of spiritual formation. Ignatius can be a wise and discerning companion on our own journey toward the embrace of our loving God. On the way, we can learn to say with him, "All for the greater glory of God!"

Meditations

The Grace of Emptiness

Theme: A pivotal point in our spiritual journey is the moment we come face-to-face with the emptiness in our heart that only God can fill.

Opening prayer: Loving God, may I always be aware that I am empty without you and totally dependent on you.

About Ignatius

Ignatius described himself at the age of twenty-six as proud, ambitious, and violent. Juan de Polanco, his secretary, added this about Ignatius as a young man: "Although much attached to the faith, he did not live in accordance with his belief, and he did not keep himself from sin. He was especially out of order in regard to gambling, matters pertaining to women, and duelling" (de Guibert, *The Jesuits: Their Spiritual Doctrine and Practice*, 23).

Then, at Pamplona, a cannonball shattered Ignatius's legs. During his long, excruciating convalescence, Ignatius underwent a change of heart, realizing the emptiness of his former life. Speaking of himself in the third person, Ignatius wrote in his autobiography:

> Our Lord assisted [Ignatius], causing other thoughts that arose from the things he read. . . . While reading the life of Our Lord and of the saints, he stopped to think, reasoning within himself, "What if I should do what St. Francis did, what St. Dominic did?" So he pondered over many things that he found to be good,

always proposing to himself what was difficult and serious, and as he proposed them, they seemed to him easy to accomplish. . . . These thoughts also lasted a good while, but when other matters intervened, the worldly thoughts . . . returned, and he also spent much time on them. . . .

Yet there was this difference. When he was thinking about the things of the world, he took much delight in them, but afterwards, when he was tired and put them aside, he found that he was dry and discontented. But when he thought of going to Jerusalem, barefoot and eating nothing but herbs and undergoing all the other rigors that he saw the saints had endured, not only was he consoled when he had these thoughts, but even after putting them aside, he remained content and happy. . . . [O]ne time his eyes were opened a little, and he began to marvel at the difference and to reflect upon it, realizing from experience that some thoughts left him sad and others happy. Little by little he came to recognize the difference between the spirits that agitated him, one from the demon, the other from God. (*Autobiography*, 23–24)

Pause: Have you ever felt the kind of emptiness or joylessness that can be filled only by God?

Ignatius's Words

Human persons are created to praise, reverence, and serve God. . . .

The other things on the face of the earth are created for us, to help us in attaining the purpose for which we are created.

Therefore, we are to make use of them insofar as they help us to attain our purpose, and we should rid ourselves of them insofar as they hinder us from attaining it.

Thus we should make ourselves indifferent to all created things, insofar as we are allowed free choice and are not under any prohibition. Consequently, as far as we are concerned, we should not prefer health to sickness, riches to poverty, honor to dishonor, a long life to a short life. The same holds for all other things.

Our one desire and choice should be what will best help us attain the purpose for which we are created.

—*The Spiritual Exercises of Saint Ignatius Loyola*, 11

Reflection

Ignatius's experience was like that of many of us who have needed to face the emptiness in our lives. Ignatius drove himself toward success, recognition, and esteem. Underlying this drive was a deep hunger and inner emptiness. Gambling, womanizing, and dueling didn't fill the void in his heart. But neither did a compulsive religiosity. After his conversion, Ignatius fasted excessively and inflicted severe penances on his body. This only whetted his inner hunger.

True conversion comes when we turn to God, acknowledging that only God can fill our emptiness and that God's love has already been poured out by Jesus. We cannot earn God's love, because Jesus gives it to us freely and constantly—if we open ourselves to it. Ignatius needed to let go and trust God. Only then could God fill the emptiness in his heart.

▶ Place in front of you a pen or pencil and some paper on which to write your reflections. If you keep a journal, have it open. Quiet yourself. Sit calmly in front of the blank paper. Breathe deeply until

you feel relaxed. Recall your experiences of emptiness, the powerful sense that something was seriously lacking in your life, the hollow ache in your heart. Then begin describing these experiences of
emptiness and inner aching. Pour out all your feelings without wor-
rying about order or grammar.

▶ Ignatius tried to fill his emptiness with gambling, womanizing,
and dueling. All of us have our own ways of filling the void we feel.
Some people overeat; others become addicted to computer games
or television. Becoming addicted to work can be a tempting way to
protect ourselves from our inner longing for God. Make an inven-
tory of your ways of hiding from the hollowness of heart that only
God can fill.

▶ Touch your own inner longings and desire for God's fullness
using this guided meditation. In preparation, darken the room so
that the only light comes from the flame of a single candle.

Sit relaxed. . . . Close your eyes. . . . Let all tension cease. . . .
Begin with your feet. . . . Feel the tension go. . . . Continue tensing
and then relaxing each part of your body. . . . Meanwhile, breathe
slowly and deeply. . . . Concentrate on your breathing for a
while. . . .

Imagine that your deepest longing, the inner ache for comple-
tion and fullness, has taken your shape and is sitting in front of
you. . . . Ask your longing what she or he really desires. . . . Listen
to her or him describe the deep longing . . . the hollow places . . .
the passion for fullness. . . .

Now, open your eyes to the light of the candle. . . . Gently pray
a word or phrase that expresses your longing: for example, "Come,"
"Light," "Jesus," or "Out of the depths, I cry to you." Repeat this
prayer word or phrase as a lamentation and as a call for God's fire
to fill you.

▶ In the silence of your heart, declare your dependence on God. Make your own act of faith to God.

From God's Word

I cannot understand my own behavior. I fail to carry out the things I want to do, and I find myself doing the very things I hate. When I act against my own will, that means I have a self that acknowledges that the Law is good, and so the thing behaving in that way is not my self but sin living in me. The fact is, I know of nothing good living in me—living, that is, in my unspiritual self—for though the will to do what is good is in me, the performance is not, with the result that instead of doing the good things I want to do, I carry out the sinful things I do not want. When I act against my will, then, it is not my true self acting, but the sin that lives in me. So, this seems to be the rule, that every single time I want to do good, something evil comes to hand. In my inmost self, I dearly love God's law, but I can see that my body follows a different law that battles against the law that my reason dictates. This is what makes me a prisoner of the law of sin that lives inside my body.

What a wretched person I am! Who will rescue me from this body doomed to death? Thanks be to God through Jesus Christ our Lord!

—Adapted from Romans 7:15–25

Closing prayer: "Help me, Lord, for I find no remedy among [creatures], yet if I thought I could find it, no labor would be too great for me. Show me, O Lord, where I may find it; even though

I should have to follow a little dog so he could help me, I would do it."

—*Autobiography*, 35

Meditation 2

A Trusting Heart

Theme: Once he learned that fullness of life can come only through a relationship with God, Ignatius trusted that God would lead him step-by-step, "just as a schoolmaster treats a child whom he is teaching." (*Autobiography*, 37)

Opening prayer: Holy Spirit, Guiding Light, I place my trust in you.

About Ignatius

While he recovered from the wounds he suffered at Pamplona and underwent his conversion, Ignatius vowed that he would make a pilgrimage to Jerusalem. True to his word, when his legs had healed sufficiently, he began his long journey. Having renounced his old ways, Ignatius took up the life of a beggar, trusting completely that God would see to his needs. After a long and dangerous trip, he reached Rome:

> There all who spoke to him, on discovering that he didn't carry any money for Jerusalem, began to dissuade him from making that trip, giving him many reasons why it was impossible to find passage without money. But he had great assurance in his soul (which he couldn't doubt) that he would find a way to go to Jerusalem. After receiving the blessing of Pope Adrian VI, he then set out for Venice eight or nine days after Easter. He had six or seven ducats which they had given him for the passage

from Venice to Jerusalem; he had accepted them, being somewhat overcome by the fears they had aroused that he would not be able to go in any other way. But two days after leaving Rome he began to realize that this was a lack of trust on his part, and it bothered him a good deal that he had accepted the ducats, so he decided it would be good to get rid of them. He finally decided to give them freely to those whom he encountered, who usually were poor. He did so, and when he arrived at Venice, he had no more than a few *quatrini* which he needed that night. (*Autobiography*, 46–47)

Ignatius "had a great certainty in his soul that God would give him the means to go to Jerusalem; this strengthened him so much that no arguments or fears suggested to him could cause him to doubt" (*Autobiography*, 47). And indeed, people took the penniless pilgrim under their care and saw to his passage to the Holy City.

Pause: How much do you trust in God's loving care for you?

Ignatius's Words

In a letter to his friend Isabel Roser, Ignatius told her to trust that even through suffering, God teaches and guides us:

In your second letter you tell me of your long-drawn-out pain in the illness you have undergone and of the great stomach pains that still remain. Indeed I cannot help feeling the liveliest sympathy with you in your sufferings, seeing that I desire every imaginable happiness and prosperity for you, provided it will help you to glorify God our Lord. And yet when we reflect, these infirmities and other temporal privations are often seen to be from God's hand to help us to a better self-knowledge and to rid ourselves of the love of created things. They help us moreover to focus our thoughts on the brevity of this life, so as to prepare for the other which has no end. When I think that in these afflictions He visits those whom He loves, I can feel no sadness or pain, because I realize that a servant of God, through an illness, turns out to be something of a doctor for the direction and the ordering of his life to God's glory and service.

—Young, *Letters of Saint Ignatius of Loyola*, 10

Reflection

Up to the time of his confinement, Ignatius had been relying totally on himself and his own resources. As he read and reflected on the life of Christ, his faith matured. He began to see that in Jesus was the truth, and he recognized that that truth could set him free (John 8:32). He entered into a personal relationship with God. His heart filled with hope.

Ignatius came to recognize that God had been leading him, that "God treated him . . . just as a schoolmaster treats a child whom he is teaching" (*Autobiography*, 37). Ignatius learned this first lesson well. He learned to trust in a thoroughly dependable God and to accept the presence and guidance of God in his life.

▶ Meditatively read "Ignatius's Words" again. Spend time listening to Ignatius speak these words to you. When you come across a passage that is especially enlightening, talk about this passage with Ignatius. Ask him and ask yourself what the passage means. When you have concluded your dialogue, write down some of your reflections.

▶ Read these words adapted from the Hebrew Scriptures: "God is a rock of strength. Creation is perfect. In all instances, God is faithful, fair, and just. . . . God made us, and we live only because God sustains us. Consider carefully your own story, the years of your past. Ask God what lessons are held in your story" (adapted from Deuteronomy 32:4–7). Consider your own story and God's faithfulness in it.

Sit quietly. Breathe deeply. Calm your soul. Write a list of at least seven key events that have shaped the course of your life. Next to each event, write your reflections about how it has been instrumental in shaping your faith and trust in God.

Then, write your reactions to these questions: How has God's hand been apparent in each event? How have good, wisdom, and growth come about because of each event?

▶ Discuss with the ever-present God how God's unfolding plan for you is becoming visible in the overall scope of your life. How have you become more hopeful? How have you felt God protecting, supporting, and leading you?

▶ In his Spiritual Exercises, Ignatius encouraged retreatants to speak with Jesus "exactly as one friend speaks to another, or as a servant speaks to a master, now asking a favor, now expressing sorrow for a wrong deed, now sharing concerns and seeking advice" (*Spiritual Exercises*, 25). Jesus is with you now. Speak with Jesus now about times when you have lost your trust in him, about areas of your life in which you need more trust, and about ways in which you resist trusting in him.

▶ Consider the story about Ignatius's trust that God would provide for him on his pilgrimage to Jerusalem. Have you contributed to the welfare of your poor sisters and brothers, trusting that God

would support you? Have you been reluctant to s}
of God's blessings to you? What practical steps
show your trust in God's faithful love for you and to care for
people?

From God's Word

Before Creation, God chose us in Christ to live whole and joyous in God's loving presence. We were adopted as God's children. God's purposes in creating us were filled with kindness. Even when we rejected God, Jesus came to show the Creator's patient love, to forgive our sins, and to urge us to lift our voices in praise of God's goodness. In short, Jesus set us free from our bondage.

Moreover, God showers us with grace, wisdom, and insight. Our eyes have been opened to the plan that God has for humankind. Everything in heaven and on earth will be brought together in unity with Jesus the Christ.

—Adapted from Ephesians 1:4–10

Closing prayer: Loving God, confirm in me my faith and trust in you. As Ignatius did, may I discover how you have been present and guiding me in all the circumstances and events of my life. Let me become aware of how, within my life, you have spoken your word. Open my heart that I may listen and hear your word of love that fills me with hope.

Meditation 3

Surrendering

Theme: At the heart of love lies only surrender, an entire gift of self that binds one irrevocably to the beloved. Ignatius was totally given, totally identified with Jesus Christ.

Opening prayer: Gracious God, I ask for the grace that I may be able to turn my will and life over to your care.

About Ignatius

In the early sixteenth century, when Ignatius was an impressionable youth, a wave of romanticism and chivalry swept over Spain. A proliferation of tales and songs conquered the Spanish imagination. One popular tale was the novel *Amadis de Gaula*. This novel and its sequels appealed to the idealism of youth:

> It became the manual of the finished caballero[,] . . . the code of honour which moulded many generations. . . . It remained throughout the sixteenth century the textbook of polite deportment, the oracle of elegant conversation, the repertory of good manners and of gallantry in forms of address. (Brodrick, *Saint Ignatius Loyola: The Pilgrim Years, 1491–1538*, 40)

Ignatius read these books avidly, filling his mind with images of chivalry and the adventures of Amadis and his son Esplandián. In Amadis, Ignatius found "the type of the perfect knight, the mirror of valour and courtesy, the pattern of loyal vassals and of constant lovers, the shield and support of the weak and necessitous, the strong arm at the service of the moral order and justice" (*Saint Ignatius Loyola*, 40).

When the moment arrived for Ignatius to turn his life over to God, to dedicate himself to Christ, he emulated Esplandián, who kept a vigil of arms before the statue of the Blessed Virgin before being invested as a knight. Ignatius described his own moment of surrender:

> [Ignatius] went on his way to Montserrat, thinking as always about the deeds he would do for the love of God. As his mind was full of ideas from Amadis de Gaul and such books, some things similar to those came to mind. Thus he decided to watch over his arms all one night, without sitting down or going to bed, but standing a while and kneeling a while, before the altar of Our Lady of Montserrat where he had resolved to leave his clothing and dress himself in the armor of Christ. . . . After arriving at Montserrat, he said a prayer and arranged for a confessor. . . . He arranged with the confessor to take his mule and to place his sword and his dagger in the church on the altar of Our Lady. . . . On the eve of the feast of Our Lady in March in the year 1522, he went at night as secretly as he could to a poor man, and stripping off all his garments he gave them to the poor man and dressed himself in his desired clothing and went to kneel before the altar of Our Lady. At times in this way, at other times standing, with his pilgrim's staff in his hand he spent the whole night. (*Autobiography*, 31–32)

The way in which Ignatius surrendered himself to God was unique to his experience. As James Brodrick explains:

> [Ignatius] is the only saint known to have dedicated himself [or herself] utterly to God by a vigil of arms. The idea had come to

him from an old romance, but the deed itself transcended all ceremony, and was an act of supernatural love, inspired by Heaven. (*Saint Ignatius Loyola*, 86)

Pause: Have you surrendered yourself to God?

Ignatius's Words

To bind oneself more to God our Lord and to show oneself generous toward Him is to consecrate oneself completely and irrevocably to His service. . . .

The more one binds himself to God our Lord and shows himself more generous toward His Divine Majesty, the more will he find God more generous toward himself and the more disposed will he be to receive graces and spiritual gifts which are greater each day.

—*The Constitutions of the Society of Jesus*, 163

Reflection

After the night at Montserrat, Ignatius was totally dedicated to God:

God was the center and preoccupation of Ignatius' thoughts, and the object of his special love, and the beloved Person for whom he wanted to do all the little acts which make up daily living. He wanted to be bound irrevocably to God, with the bridges burnt which might lead back to another way of living in which he might have interests other than God—God and [all others] for whom Jesus Christ had shed His blood. (*Constitutions*, 15)

At the point of surrender, we, like Ignatius, stop playing God. We realize that God guides the universe, not us. We are held in the palm of God's hand. To attain a measure of peace and serenity in our lives, we need to make a decisive step in which we turn our lives over to God. We rest in God's embrace. We surrender and entrust the outcome to God.

By surrendering, we live centered in the present time, knowing that God will tell us what we need to know if we but listen to our experience and trust God's actions. In a stance of ongoing surrender to God, we will be restored to fullness of trust in God, in ourselves, and in others.

▶ Read "Ignatius's Words" slowly and meditatively again. Pick a thought that seems particularly challenging or consoling to you. Stay with this thought, pondering its significance for you.

▶ Have you ever felt powerless to control some compulsion or drive within yourself? Ponder areas of your life that seem uncontrollable without God's help: maybe long-standing anger at someone or yourself, maybe a compulsion to shine or perform in groups, perhaps a drive to succeed in all situations, or perhaps a desire always to be needed. As you get in touch with your powerlessness, remember that God already knows your inmost being and loves you unconditionally. Talk to God about your powerlessness. Are you willing to surrender these compulsions to God's care and leave yourself open to God's grace and power?

▶ Write a list of all the wonderful gifts God has bestowed on you: intimate friendships, good deeds, positive contributions to your family or community, and so on. Discuss these gifts with God. Is it easy to surrender them to God? Ask God if you really deserved these gifts and why they were bestowed on you.

▶ Ponder this question: Which parts of my life am I unwilling to surrender to God's will?

▶ Write a list of ways your life would improve if you surrendered to God's will.

▶ Write your own prayer of surrender to God. Compose it so that it surrenders to God's will your compulsions, gifts, fears, and achievements. Pray this prayer frequently, but especially when you feel powerless—or particularly powerful. Your prayer can remind you that God is the center of your life.

▶ Ignatius ritualized his surrender by keeping a vigil of arms before the statue of Mary. Create a ritual of your own that makes concrete your surrender to God's will; then make your surrender. Keep some visible symbol of your decision to turn your life over to God; when you need a reminder of your surrender, ponder this symbol.

From God's Word

I believe nothing can happen that will outweigh the supreme advantage of knowing Christ Jesus. . . . For him I have accepted the loss of everything, and I look on everything as so much rubbish if only I can have Christ and be given a place in him. I am no longer trying for perfection by my own efforts, the perfection that comes from the Law, but I want only the perfection that comes through faith in Christ and is from God and based on faith. All I want is to know Christ and the power of his resurrection and to share his sufferings by reproducing the pattern of his death. That is the way I can hope to take my place in the resurrection of the dead. Not that I have become perfect yet: I have not yet won, but I am still running, trying to capture the prize for which Christ Jesus captured me. I can assure you, I am far from thinking that I have already won. All I can say is that I forget the past and

I strain ahead for what is still to come; I am racing for the finish, for the prize to which God calls us upward to receive in Christ Jesus. We who are called perfect must all think in this way. If you see things differently on some point, God will make it clear to you; meanwhile, let us go forward on the road that has brought us to where we are.

—Adapted from Philippians 3:7–16

Closing prayer: "Take, Lord, and receive all my liberty, my memory, my understanding, and my entire will, all that I have and possess. You have given all to me. To you, Lord, I return it. All is yours. Dispose of it wholly according to your will. Give me your love and your grace. That is enough for me."

—*Spiritual Exercises*, 79

Meditation 4

Radical Honesty

Theme: To turn toward God, Ignatius first needed to confront truthfully his sinfulness, emptiness, and dependence on God. Ignatius committed himself to radical honesty.

Opening prayer:

> God, search me and know my heart;
> probe me and know my thoughts.
> Make sure I do not follow evil ways,
> and guide me in the way of life eternal.
> —Psalm 139:23–24, from *Psalms Anew: In Inclusive Language*

About Ignatius

During his extended period of recuperation from the injuries to his legs, Ignatius became painfully aware not only of his physical frailty but also of his moral frailty. Thoughts of glory and pleasure that had pleased him before he was wounded now left him sad and disturbed. These discouraging thoughts humbled him:

> [H]e began to think more earnestly about his past life and about the great need he had to do penance for it. At this point the desire to imitate the saints came to him, though he gave no thought to the circumstances, but only promised with God's grace to do as they had done. (*Autobiography*, 24)

Ignatius began the honest and thorough examination of his life that would lead to his radical commitment to Jesus. As part of his spiritual recovery, he pledged to make a pilgrimage to Jerusalem. His family strongly opposed his journey, but Ignatius would not budge:

> His brother took him from one room to another and with many protestations begged him not to throw himself away and to consider what hopes had been placed in him and what he could become and he advanced other similar arguments, all with the purpose of dissuading him from his good intention. But he answered in such a way that, without departing from the truth, for he was now very scrupulous about that, he evaded his brother. (*Autobiography*, 26)

Ignatius recognized that to truly reform himself, he had to be honest with himself and other people.

Early in his pilgrimage, Ignatius took another step of radical honesty. At Montserrat, with deep humility of heart, Ignatius encountered the truth and full weight of his sinfulness. "He said a prayer and arranged for a confessor. He made a general confession in writing which lasted three days" (*Autobiography*, 31). Although later plagued by scruples, Ignatius had embarked on his path to holiness by being completely honest with himself before God.

Pause: How are you being drawn to greater honesty about your thoughts, feelings, words, and actions and their ramifications?

Ignatius's Words

For the entire first week in the four weeks of the Spiritual Exercises, Ignatius directed retreatants to meditate on their sinfulness and to prepare for forgiveness. Consistent with the call of John the Baptist to acknowledge and repent of our sin so that we can turn to Christ, Ignatius urged retreatants to do likewise. In the second exercise of the first week, Ignatius gave these instructions:

First Point. This is the review of my sins. I will call to mind all the sins of my life, year by year and period by period. Three things will help me in this: first to remember the place and house where I lived; second, my relationships with others; third, the positions I have held.

Second Point. This is to weigh the gravity of my sins and see the ugliness and malice. . . .

Fourth Point. This is to consider who God is against whom I have sinned, reflecting on the divine attributes and comparing them with their contraries in me: God's wisdom with my ignorance, God's omnipotence with my weakness, God's justice with my iniquity, God's goodness with my sinfulness.

Fifth Point. This is a cry of wonder with growing emotion as I consider all creatures. How have they permitted me to live and sustained me in life? . . . Why have the heavens, sun, moon, stars and elements, the fruits, birds, fishes and animals, served my needs? Why has the earth not opened up and swallowed me up, condemning me to eternal separation from God?

Colloquy. I will conclude with a colloquy, praising the mercy of God our Lord, pouring out my thoughts and giving thanks to the Lord for granting me life up to this moment. I will resolve with the help of God's grace to amend for the future.

—Spiritual Exercises, 26–27

At the end of the four weeks of the exercises, Ignatius urged retreatants to be just as honest in acknowledging the many gifts that God has showered on them and in recognizing what they have to share with other people.

Reflection

Honesty is an integral part of humility, which means saying yes to our humanness, accepting both the agony and the ecstasy of our creaturehood. We are of the earth—*humus*—and are called to embrace the totality of who we are. To accept our limitations and fulfill our potential takes courage. Humility—accepting the truth—requires honesty.

Honesty and humility demand surrender or a letting go of our desire for control, security, esteem, and approval. Honesty and humility call us to reflect, as Ignatius did, on the patterns of our life that deflect us from the way of Christ. Thus, the examination of conscience became integral to the spirituality of Ignatius. He encouraged those who came to him for direction and confession to persist in a thorough examination of their soul. This examination of conscience that Ignatius developed and expanded as the examen of consciousness is basic and foundational for authentic inner healing.

Ignatius identified and named his sinfulness on the way to aligning his intention with the intention of God present within him. Only God's love and grace made this possible.

This same love and grace is available to us. With confidence in God's help, we can look forward to the freedom brought by God's forgiveness and by honesty with ourselves.

▶ Read again the story of Ignatius's repentance in "About Ignatius." Ignatius's brother tried to turn him away from radical conversion to Christ. Do any people, situations, or internal conflicts hinder an honest examination and reform of your life?

▶ Make an examination of the state of your soul. You may find it helpful to write your examen of consciousness in your journal. To focus your meditation, place a crucifix or an icon of the crucified Jesus before you. Quiet yourself in body and spirit. Remind yourself that the God of love dwells within you. Declare your dependency on God and ask for the grace you most desire as you enter this process of examining your life. Speak to Jesus as friend to friend. Invite him into your heart. Recall that Jesus gave his life for you. Then, begin your examination either using the steps outlined in "Ignatius's Words" or using these questions:

- Have I allowed myself to believe that Jesus loves me as I am?
- How have I responded to Christ's love for me?
- How am I responding to Christ's love now?
- Has my need for control, the esteem of other people, or security undermined my commitment to the good news?
- Have I been honest with myself about my compulsions and failings?
- Have I tried to replace dependence on God's love with the acquiring of wealth, property, degrees, acquaintances, awards, and so on?
- Have I kept in touch with my feelings, and do I know what resides in my heart?
- Do I make time to pray and meditate to keep my focus on living in the way of Jesus?
- In what other ways do I depart from trusting in God's love and living a life of love for my sisters and brothers?
- What talents, qualities, and skills has God given me?

- What other blessings has God showered upon me?
- How have I expressed my thanksgiving to the Creator?

Converse with Jesus about one or two situations in your present life about which you feel anxiety, shame, or anger—situations in which you would like to act more Christlike.

Pray a litany of thanksgiving for all the gifts God has bestowed upon you.

▶ Pray "A Private Litany of Humility," which follows, reflecting on each phrase and its meaning for you:

From the desire of being praised, deliver me, Jesus.
From the desire of being honored, deliver me, Jesus.
From the desire of being preferred, deliver me, Jesus.
From the desire of being consulted, deliver me, Jesus.
From the desire of being approved, deliver me, Jesus.
From the desire of comfort and ease, deliver me, Jesus.
From the fear of being criticized, deliver me, Jesus.
From the fear of being passed over, deliver me, Jesus.
From the fear of being forgotten, deliver me, Jesus.
From the fear of being lonely, deliver me, Jesus.
From the fear of being hurt, deliver me, Jesus.
From the fear of suffering, deliver me, Jesus.
Jesus, meek and humble of heart,
Make my strength like unto Thine. Amen.

—*Orientations*, volume 1, 108

From God's Word

In your goodness, O God, have mercy on me;
with gentleness wipe away my faults.

Cleanse me of guilt;
   free me from my sins.
My faults are always before me;
   my sins haunt my mind.
I have sinned against you and no other—
   knowing that my actions were wrong in your eyes.
Until I am clean, bathe me with hyssop;
   wash me until I am whiter than snow.
Infuse me with joy and gladness;
Create a pure heart in me, O my God;
   renew me with a steadfast spirit.

—Psalm 51:1–10, *Psalms Anew*

Closing prayer: Jesus, meek and humble of heart, make my heart like yours.

Meditation 5

Obeying God's Will

Theme: Obedience to the spirit of Jesus shaped Ignatius's life. The qualities of availability, mobility, and inclusiveness were marks of his obedience.

Opening prayer: Gracious God, give me an obedient heart. Open my ears so that I will always listen and respond to you in all the circumstances of my life.

About Ignatius

Early in his spiritual journey, Ignatius learned this lesson: obedience is better than sacrifice (1 Samuel 15:22). After his surrender to God, he learned obedience through his struggle with scruples:

> Even though the general confession he had made at Montserrat had been made with enough care and had been completely written, as has been said, still at times it seemed to him that he had not confessed certain things. This caused him much distress, because although he confessed it, he was not satisfied. Thus he began to look for some spiritual men who could cure him of these scruples, but nothing helped him. At last a very spiritual man, a doctor of the cathedral who preached there, told him one day in confession to write down everything he could remember. He did so, but after confession the scruples still returned and each time in more detail so that he was very troubled. Although he realized that those scruples did him much harm and that it

29

would be wise to be rid of them, he could not do that himself. Sometimes he thought it might cure him if his confessor would order him in the name of Jesus Christ not to confess anything from the past; he wanted his confessor to direct him thus, but he did not dare say so to his confessor.

But without his saying so, his confessor ordered him not to confess anything from the past, unless it should be something very clear. But inasmuch as he thought all those things were very clear, this order was of no benefit to him, and so he continued with his difficulty. . . . [M]any months had now passed since [his scruples] had begun to torment him. . . .

Then there came to his mind the story of a saint who, in order to obtain something from God that he wanted very much, went without eating many days until he got it. Thinking about this for a good while, he at last decided to do it, telling himself that he would not eat or drink until God took care of him or until he saw that death was indeed near; for if he saw that he was at that point where he would have to die if he did not eat, then he would decide to ask for bread and to eat (as if at that point he could in fact ask for it or eat it).

This happened one Sunday after he had received communion; he persevered the whole week without putting anything into his mouth nor ceasing to do his usual exercises, even going to divine office and saying his prayers on his knees, even at midnight and so forth. But when the next Sunday came and he had to go to confession, because he used to tell his confessor in very great detail what he had done, he also told him how he had eaten nothing during that week. His confessor ordered him to break off his abstinence; though he still felt strong he obeyed his confessor and that day and the next felt free from scruples. (*Autobiography*, 34–36)

Pause: Consider your feelings about the word *obedience*. What place does obedience have in your lifestyle?

Ignatius's Words

In a letter to his Jesuit brothers, Ignatius wrote the following:

It is in obedience more than in any other [virtue] that God our Lord gives me the desire to see you become outstanding, not only for the particular good to be found in it, as the Holy Scripture so praised with examples and words in the Old and the New Testament, but because (as St. Gregory says) . . . "obedience is a virtue that by itself imprints in the soul all the other virtues, and once printed, it keeps them there." For as long as obedience blooms, all other virtues will also be seen to be blooming and bear the fruit that I wish for your souls, which is the same desired by Him. He redeemed, out of obedience, a world lost for lack of it. . . .

I pray to you, for the love of Christ our Lord, that not only ordered obedience, but preceded with His example of obedience, that . . . the knowledge and true love of God our Lord may entirely possess and guide your soul through this pilgrimage to lead you, with many others through your means, to the ultimate and most happy end of His eternal happiness.

—*Antonio T. de Nicolas, Powers of Imagining: Ignatius de Loyola*, 303, 311

Reflection

The word *obedience* comes from a Latin word meaning "to listen." Ignatius listened to God speaking through his confessor and in his own heart. When he obeyed—freely surrendered his will to that of God—Ignatius's heart underwent a transformation. After all, God's will is that we love God, our sisters and brothers, and ourselves. When Ignatius obeyed his confessor, thus freeing himself from his scruples, he realized God's love for him. This event became a touchstone for Ignatius's entire life. In his story, we see many other examples of Ignatius's listening to and following of God's will.

Through Ignatius's obedience, the fullness of the Spirit could act within him. Paradoxically, as Ignatius submitted to the will of God spoken through the Scriptures, spiritual advisers, church authorities, his experiences, and in his own heart, he could take each step of his spiritual journey with confidence.

▶ How do we listen for God's will? When do we know to obey? Remember that God wills that we love and be loved, that we be filled with faith and hope, and that we come to fullness of life. Ask yourself the following questions, and then write your answers for each, letting ideas and examples flow freely from your memory, imagination, and understanding:

- Who are all the people I love and who love me?
- In what and in whom do I have faith? What are the stars of faith that lead me through life?
- What are the sources of my hope? What gives me an expectancy that somehow, ultimately, all will be well?
- Have I seen my response to these people and sources of love, faith, and hope as obedience to God's holy will?
- When have I turned aside from obeying God's call to love? To believe? To be hopeful?

In prayer, thank God for the times you have obeyed God's will to love, to believe, and to be filled with hope. Ask God's pardon for the times you have disobeyed God's will.

Reflect on ways in which you can be more obedient to God's will, and resolve to listen and obey more wholeheartedly.

▶ Make a list of the people to whom you are called to obedience. How has God's will been revealed in your submission?

▶ Ignatius introduced into his Jesuit community a practice called *manifestation of conscience*. Each member of the community was supposed to commit himself to share openly with his superior all his joys, sufferings, successes, and failures. In this same spirit, share with a trustworthy and wise person the experience of your own obedience, your resistance, your failures, and the gifts you have received in willing obedience.

▶ Draw a picture of a garden. In the center of your garden, draw a symbol for obedience. Around the symbol, sketch other symbols that represent your experience of obedience.

▶ Reflect on your drawing. How do you see your feelings about obedience represented in your drawing? Is the fruit of your obedience evident? Title your drawing with a quotation from Scripture that embraces the call and meaning of obedience for you. Invite Jesus to walk through your garden with you. Share and enjoy the fruit of your garden with Jesus.

From God's Word

In the days of his flesh, Jesus offered up prayers and supplications, with loud cries and tears, to the one who was able to save him from death, and he was heard because of his reverent submission. Although he was a Son, he learned obedience through what he suffered; and having been made perfect, he became the source of eternal salvation for all who obey him, having been designated by God a high priest according to the order of Melchizedek.

—Hebrews 5:7–10

Closing prayer: "Fill us, we pray, [God], with your light and life that we may show forth your wondrous glory. Grant that your love may so fill our lives that we may count nothing too small to do for you, nothing too much to give and nothing too hard to bear."

—Prayer of Ignatius of Loyola

Meditation 6

Passionate Union with Christ

Theme: Ignatius lived intimately and passionately centered in Christ. Gradually, every moment became a response to Christ's invitation to be *mecum*, that is, "with me."

Opening prayer: Loving God, may I always hear your voice within my heart and respond to your invitation to oneness with you: "Arise, my love, my fair one, and come away" (Song of Songs 2:10).

About Ignatius

God acknowledged Ignatius's great love while "the pilgrim" made his way to Rome for the second and last time in his life:

> After [Ignatius] became a priest he had decided to spend a year without saying mass, preparing himself and begging Our Lady to deign to place him with her Son. One day, while still a few miles from Rome, he was praying in a church [at La Storta] and experienced such a change in his soul and saw so clearly that God the Father had placed him with His Son Christ that his mind could not doubt that God the Father had indeed placed him with His Son. (*Autobiography*, 89)
>
> With deep feeling Ignatius perceived himself as one intimately united with Christ; and he also desired that the society [of Jesus] which was soon to be founded [by him] should be totally dedicated to Him and bear His name. (de Dalmases, *Ignatius of Loyola, Founder of the Jesuits*, 153)

The experience of mystical acceptance and confirmation at La Storta would continue to be significant for Ignatius. He frequently referred to it in his diary and other writings. The vision served as a frame of reference and source of consolation. For example, while writing in his diary about a decision regarding the practice of poverty for the Jesuit community, Ignatius said that he gained confidence from the vision, with these thoughts growing in intensity and seeming to be a confirmation, even though [he] received no consolations about this matter, and Jesus' showing himself, or letting himself be felt, seeming to [him] to be somehow the work of the Most Holy Trinity, and remembering when the Father placed [him] with his Son. (Dunphy, *Placed with Jesus Bearing His Cross*, 337)

Ignatius outlined this last entry in a box, as he did with all the passages he deemed particularly important.

Pause: Does the example of Ignatius speak to your own desire for intimate union with Christ?

Ignatius's Words

In instructing new members of the Society of Jesus, Ignatius said the following:

It is likewise highly important to . . . accept and desire with all possible energy whatever Christ our Lord has loved and embraced. Just as the men of the world who follow the world love and seek with such great diligence honors, fame, and esteem for a great name on earth, as the world teaches them, so those who are progressing in the spiritual life and truly following Christ our Lord love and intensely desire . . . to clothe themselves with the same clothing and uniform of their Lord because of the love and reverence which He deserves, to such an extent that where there would be no offense to His Divine Majesty and no imputation of sin to the neighbor, they would wish to suffer injuries, false accusations, and affronts, and to be held and esteemed as fools (but without their giving any occasion for this), because of their desire to resemble and imitate in some manner our Creator and Lord Jesus Christ, by putting on His clothing and uniform, since it was for our spiritual profit that He clothed Himself as He did. For He gave us an example that in all things possible to us we might seek, through the aid of His grace, to imitate and follow Him, since He is the way which leads men to life.

—*Constitutions*, 107–108

Reflection

Jesus Christ calls all Christians into union with him. God gives us the same grace given to Ignatius at La Storta—that is, to put on Christ, to live all of life in his way, and to orient all our actions according to the example of Jesus given in the New Testament and through the action of the Spirit within us.

Ignatius originally chose the name Company of Jesus for his followers. The name is rooted in Ignatius's conviction that he and his companions had been called to live "a life of service to God with Christ, through Christ, in Christ, and as Christ" (de Guibert, *Jesuits*, 39).

All of us have been invited to be companions of Jesus. God chose us. We belong in the embrace of God's love just as Jesus does. Even though we, like Ignatius, may suffer from struggles small or great, ultimately God will sustain us if we but see and accept God's sustenance.

▶ Contemplate an icon or image of Christ while you do the following:

Relax your body. Breathe deeply. Focus on the icon or image. Look deeply into the eyes of Christ. Listen to the deepest desire of your heart. Reflect on the words of Jesus to his disciples: "Who do people say that I am?" (Mark 8:27).

How do you answer Jesus? Who does your life say that Christ is?

▶ In the Second Week of the Spiritual Exercises, Ignatius invites us to make explicit our desire to be totally united with Christ. In the exercise called "The Two Standards," we are instructed to consider how Christ draws men and women to the fullness of life as opposed to the way Satan, the enemy of our human nature, binds and enslaves us. To show your desire to be one with Christ, pray in the following way:

- Begin by asking God for an understanding of and desire for the way of life that Jesus taught us.

- Bringing to mind stories and parables from the New Testament, ponder the message that Jesus taught to his followers through both his words and example. To what did Jesus invite people? Was his manner one of command or of gentle inspiration?

- Ask Mary to intercede for you: that you will receive the gift of total dependency on God. Ask that you would be so detached from all things that you would put all your talents, possessions, and achievements at the service of Christ. Pray to follow in the pattern of Christ's life, even to the end. Providing it would not be sinful on anyone's part, pray that if it is God's wish for you, you will have, like Christ, the courage and strength to endure poverty and personal humiliation. Then, pray the Hail Mary.

- In the company of Mary, approach Jesus and offer the same prayer: that he obtain for you the same graces from God. Then, slowly, pausing to reflect on the meaning of each phrase, pray the following prayer, Soul of Christ:

Jesus, may all that is you flow into me.
May your body and blood be my food and drink.
May your passion and death be my strength and life.
Jesus, with you by my side enough has been given.
May the shelter I seek be the shadow of your cross.
Let me not run from the love which you offer,
But hold me safe from the forces of evil.
On each of my dyings shed your light and your love.
Keep calling to me until that day comes,
When, with your saints, I may praise you forever. Amen.

—Fleming, *Hearts on Fire*, 3

▶ In the presence of Jesus and Mary—and remembering that they offer you to God—approach God. Again, make the same request for the grace to be totally united with Christ. Pray the Our Father.

Throughout your day, pray these words of Ignatius: "Through Christ, in Christ, and as Christ."

From God's Word

You have stripped off the old self with its practices and have clothed yourselves with the new self, which is being renewed in knowledge according to the image of its creator. In that renewal there is no longer Greek and Jew, circumcised and uncircumcised, barbarian, Scythian, slave and free; but Christ is all and in all!

As God's chosen ones, holy and beloved, clothe yourselves with compassion, kindness, humility, meekness, and patience. Bear with one another and, if anyone has a complaint against another, forgive each other; just as the Lord has forgiven you, so you also must forgive. Above all, clothe yourselves with love, which binds everything together in perfect harmony. And let the peace of Christ rule in your hearts, to which indeed you were called in the one body. And be thankful.

—Colossians 3:9–15

Closing prayer: "Eternal [God], confirm me; Eternal Son, confirm me; Eternal Spirit, confirm me; Holy Trinity, confirm me; my only God, confirm me!"

—*The Spiritual Journal of Saint Ignatius Loyola, February 1544–1545*, 12

Meditation 7

Compassionate Friendship

Theme: Whereas history portrays Ignatius as the general of an "army," those who were close to him described a man of tender compassion who had a gift for friendship and for encouraging the same caring fellowship among his first companions.

Opening prayer: Jesus, you call us friends. You invite us to love one another as you have loved us. Create among us unity of mind in truth and oneness of heart in charity.

About Ignatius

The Society of Jesus began as a gathering of friends in Jesus' name. The memories of that first generation portrayed Ignatius as a loving friend to them:

> Ignatius's manner of governing was based on the fatherly love which he had for his sons. He made no distinctions, to such a point that each one felt himself to be the object of "the Father's" strong liking.
>
> He knew how to blend strictness with gentleness. Câmara [who recorded Ignatius's autobiography] says that Ignatius inclined more to the side of love and that was why he was so much loved by all. Câmara added that he did not know anyone in the Society who did not have a great love for him and did not feel himself loved by the Father.

He tended to put a good interpretation on the actions of others, so much so that "the Father's interpretations" became a proverbial phrase.

He promoted every means helpful to the union that ought to reign among all. One of those was the community recreations. He was once asked whether the recreation ought not to be dropped on fast days, since there was no supper. He answered that the recreation was held not only to avoid injury to health by study right after the meal, but also that the brothers might deal with one another and thus come to that mutual knowledge and esteem and to foster charity (Dalmases, *Ignatius of Loyola*, 257–258).

Sebastiano Romei, rector of the Roman College, said that in his time great joy was prevalent among all the members of the community, because Ignatius by his presence and conversation brought life to them all (Dalmases, 260).

[Ignatius] welcomed all with affection; and when he wanted to give someone special delight, he seemed to be trying to take him into his very heart. Once when he wished to give an embrace of welcome to a Flemish youth who had just arrived and who was very tall, Ignatius, who was small in stature, leaped up to reach the young man's neck (Dalmases, 261).

Pause: Consider the gentleness and sensitivity of Ignatius's love for his companions. In your relationships, how do you see the presence or absence of these qualities?

Ignatius's Words

In the Constitutions for the Jesuits, Ignatius outlined ways of uniting the members of his community who were spread throughout the world:

The more difficult it is for the members of this congregation to be united with their head and among themselves, since they are so scattered among the faithful and among the unbelievers in diverse regions of the world, the more ought means to be sought for that union. For the Society cannot be preserved, or governed, or, consequently, attain the end it seeks for the greater glory of God unless its members are united among themselves and with their head. Therefore the present treatise will deal first with what can aid the union of hearts. . . .

The chief bond to cement the union of the members among themselves and with their head is, on both sides, the love of God our Lord. For when the superior and the subjects are closely united to His Divine and Supreme Goodness, they will very easily be united among themselves, through that same love which will descend from the Divine Goodness and spread to all other men, and particularly into the body of the Society. Thus from both sides charity will come to further this union between superiors and subjects, and in general all goodness and virtues through which one proceeds in conformity with the spirit. . . .

Still another great help can be found in uniformity, both interior uniformity of doctrine, judgments, and wills, as far as this is possible . . ., and exterior uniformity in respect to clothing, ceremonies of the Mass, and other such matters, to the extent that the different qualities of persons, places, and the like, permit.

—*Constitutions*, 285, 291

Reflection

Ignatius nurtured his brothers with his love. With the tenderness of a father, he displayed a sincere interest in each companion, accepting each one in his uniqueness. He was consistent in offering encouragement and support, remaining attentive to their individual needs.

Ignatius not only nurtured a close relationship between himself and each companion, he also fostered a mutual union of hearts in a community marked by diversity. From the beginning, the companions represented many nationalities. They engaged in many different missions and were scattered throughout the known world. Ignatius encouraged diligence in the nurturing of friendship and frequent communication among them.

The original community made a point of coming together at regular intervals to share a common meal, to talk of spiritual matters, and to discuss their problems. Ignatius and his companions in this way preserved themselves, and "they diverted themselves and gave themselves heart to press on with their good intentions" (Osuna, *Friends in the Lord*, 61).

Jesus called all Christians to build community through mutual concern, compassion, sharing, and the development of friendships. Indeed, in the very beginnings of the church, people pointed to the

Christians and remarked on how they loved one another. Compassionate friendships support, affirm, and invite us to full life in Christ.

▶ Name the persons who make up your community, your friends in the Lord. These may be members of your family, religious community, parish community, network of friends, or support group. Now, consider the following questions:

- What do you do to nourish love and foster life-giving relationships with these persons?
- How do you cope with differences, diversity, and distance?
- Are you content with the degree to which you experience a "union of hearts" in these relationships? What can you do to enhance the quality of love within them?
- From whom do you desire to ask forgiveness for your negligence in a relationship? To whom do you need to make amends?

Pray for each member of your community and for the grace to continue building each relationship and the community.

▶ Ignatius uniquely integrated the qualities of gentleness and strength. A person of great flexibility, he adjusted himself to the personalities and needs of others. When it came to directing or correcting another, he possessed a loving intuition with regard to the other's strength, sensitivity, or fragility, and he was a master at fitting the reprimand or direction to that particular individual.

Bring to mind two people: one close friend and one person with whom you have trouble relating. Then, prayerfully ponder these questions about each relationship:

- Am I sensitive to the emotions of _____ ?
- How do I deal with my differences with _____ ?

- What practical steps do I take to further develop my relationship with _____?
- What does my relationship with _____ offer me?
- What do I offer _____?

Discuss each relationship with Jesus, asking for the grace you need to love each person.

▶ Recall the incident described in "About Ignatius" when he leaped to embrace the young man. Ask yourself, "How spontaneous and free am I in expressing my affection to those I love?" Then, pray for the grace to muster up the courage you need to be spontaneous, demonstrative, and generous with your love.

▶ Write a letter or phone a friend or family member who lives far away. When you have sent the letter or finished the call, pray for this friend or relative.

From God's Word

How good it is, how pleasant,
for God's people to live in unity.
It is like the precious oil
running down from Aaron's head and beard,
down to the collar of his robes.
It is like the dew on Mount Hermon
falling on the hills of Zion.
For there Yahweh has promised a blessing,
life that never ends.

—Psalm 133, *Psalms Anew*

Closing prayer: "I confess, my God, that I have long been, and even now am, recalcitrant to the love of my neighbour. . . . Grant, O God, that the light of your countenance may shine for me in the life of that 'other.' . . . Grant that I may see you, even and above all, in the souls of my brothers, at their most personal, and most true, and most distant."

—Pierre Teilhard de Chardin, *The Divine Milieu*, 145

Meditation 8

All for God's Greater Glory

Theme: The "greater glory of God" motivated Ignatius's life. He always reached for "the more."

Opening prayer: Loving and generous God, instill within my heart a holy restlessness so that I am never satisfied with less than you and your will.

About Ignatius

During his convalescence from the wounds taken at Pamplona, Ignatius read the lives of the saints and was especially inspired by Francis of Assisi and Dominic. These saints kindled the fires of commitment in Ignatius. He hungered to do great deeds for the glory of God. This total dedication to the greater glory of God was soon tested.

In Salamanca, Ignatius began teaching religion to those who would listen. Suspicious of Ignatius because he had not been properly trained in theology, the local church authorities jailed him for interrogation. During his imprisonment, many people came to visit him. When asked by a distinguished visitor how he fared, Ignatius replied:

"I will answer what I answered today to a lady who, on seeing me in prison, spoke words of compassion." [He] said to her, "By this you show that you do not wish to be imprisoned for the love of God. Does imprisonment seem to be such a great evil to you?

49

Well, I will tell you that there are not so many grills and chains in Salamanca that I would not wish for more for the love of God." (*Autobiography*, 70)

After twenty-two days, Ignatius was freed from prison but prohibited from catechizing on certain subjects.

He found great difficulty in remaining in Salamanca, for in the matter of helping souls it seemed to him that the door had been closed by this prohibition. . . .

[T]he same desire that he had to help souls, and for that reason to study first and to gather some others for the same purpose and to keep those he had, did not fail him. Resolving to go to Paris, he arranged with [his companions] to wait there while he went to see if he could find some means by which they could study.

Many important persons strongly insisted that he should not go, but they could never dissuade him. . . . When he arrived at Barcelona all those who knew him advised him against the journey to France because of the great wars there, recounting many specific examples, even telling him that they put Spaniards on roasting spits, but he never had any kind of fear. (*Autobiography*, 70–71)

Pause: Which heroes and heroines have inspired you to go beyond yourself to build the reign of God?

Ignatius's Words

Ignatius's zeal led him to seek the greater glory of God. This vital force of his life is conveyed in "The Call of Christ the King," which appears at the beginning of the Second

Week of the Spiritual Exercises. Having asked us to reflect on the call of earthly rulers, Ignatius leads us to consider the reign of Christ:

First Point. If such a call of an earthly leader to the people deserves our attention, how much more worthy of consideration is Christ our eternal Lord, before whom stands the entire world. Christ calls all people, and to each individual he addresses these words: "It is my will to serve the whole world, conquering all evil through love, and thus to enter the glory of God. Therefore, whoever wishes to come with me must be willing to labor with me, that by following me in suffering, you may follow me in glory."

Second Point. Consider that all persons who have good judgment and reason will offer themselves entirely for this work.

Third Point. Those who wish to give greater proof of their love, and to distinguish themselves in the service of the eternal and universal Lord, will not only offer themselves entirely for this work, but will act against their own sensuality and love for the flesh and the world, and make offerings of greater value and importance in words such as these:

Eternal Lord of All. Eternal Lord of all, in the presence of your infinite goodness, and of your glorious mother, and of all the saints of heaven, I make this offering of myself with your grace and help. It is my fervent desire and deliberate choice, provided only that it is for your greater service and praise, to imitate you in bearing all wrong, all abuse and all poverty, both actual and spiritual, should you deign to choose me and admit me to such a state and way of life.

—*Spiritual Exercises*, 36

Reflection

As a child, Ignatius listened with amazement while his father and his eldest brother told stories about how their ancestors had served with distinction the kings of Castile, how they had identified with and dedicated themselves to the monarchy, and how they had been richly rewarded for their devotion. After his conversion, Ignatius strove to serve the greater glory of the one true ruler of the world: Christ.

Human rulers have human flaws. They can be greedy or profligate, brutal or weak, arbitrary or narrow, petty or insensitive. Nonetheless, most of us follow these human rulers.

Ignatius reminded us that the only ruler truly deserving of our total dedication is Jesus Christ. Only Jesus merits our complete attention, obedience, service, and worship. Only Jesus gives unconditional love, is eternally faithful, and is the best source of hope. In the Exercises, Ignatius invited us to enter Christ's service wholeheartedly. If we can serve human rulers well, we should serve Christ without reserve.

▶ Brainstorm. Write a list of all the ways you follow human leaders or rulers. Write the names of the human leaders and rulers to whom you offer obedience and service. Indicate in some way the level of respect, service, or honor that each leader deserves. Think about each one's flaws and positive contributions.

Finally, ponder this question: Do I pay more attention to obeying human rulers than I do to following the call of Christ?

▶ Slowly read "Ignatius's Words" again. Then meditate on each point from the Spiritual Exercises listed there. Offer the prayer contained in the third point; pray it slowly, meditating on each phrase. How does it apply to you?

▶ Ignatius was consumed with the honor and the glory of God. He would do, sacrifice, or suffer anything for the coming of God's reign. Consider these questions about your focus in life:

- What focuses your energies? What consumes you?
- How can you relate what consumes you or gives your life focus to the call of Christ—the Good News?

▶ Like the mythological heroes and heroines of old, Ignatius gave his life for someone and for something beyond himself. Like the saints who had inspired him, Ignatius consecrated himself to Christ.

- What does the call of Christ stir within you?
- What "grills and chains" do you suffer for the love of Christ?
- What chains within you shackle the stirrings you may feel to follow Jesus more completely?
- Where are you being stretched to be more than your culture or family has programmed you to be? To do things you never dreamed possible?
- What will you do to live freely in Christ, to love generously, to forgive magnanimously, and to serve with joy even your enemies?

Once again, pray the prayer in the third point in "Ignatius's Words":

Eternal Lord of All. Eternal Lord of all, in the presence of your infinite goodness, and of your glorious mother, and of all the saints of heaven, I make this offering of myself with your grace and help. It is my fervent desire and deliberate choice, provided only that it is for your greater service and praise, to imitate you in bearing all wrong, all abuse and all poverty, both actual and spiritual, should you deign to choose me and admit me to such a state and way of life.

From God's Word

Jesus drew the people and his disciples together and said, "If people want to follow me, they must turn away from selfishness, bear their crosses, and follow after me. People who seek to save themselves will lose their souls. People who sacrifice themselves for me, or for the Gospel, will save their souls. Finally, what good is it to rule the world but lose eternal life? And indeed what can people offer in exchange for their lives?"

—Adapted from Mark 8:34–37

Closing prayer: Teach us, O God, to serve you as you deserve; to give and not to count the cost; to fight and not to notice the wounds; to toil and not to look for rest; to labor and not to ask for any reward, except that of knowing that we do your will through Jesus Christ our Lord.

—Adapted from "Obedience," in *The Oxford Book of Prayer*, 86

Meditation 9

Discerning God's Will

Theme: With ever-greater sensitivity, Ignatius learned to read the movements within his heart, those that drew him to Christ and those that tended to lead him away from his authentic goal.

Opening prayer: "[Christ], I need your Spirit, that divine force that has transformed so many human personalities, making them capable of extraordinary deeds and extraordinary lives. Give me that Spirit which, coming from You and going to You, infinite Holiness, is a Holy Spirit."

—Pedro Arrupe, *Challenge to Religious Life Today*, 295

About Ignatius

Many people wrote Ignatius to ask for his guidance. A response that Ignatius sent to Sister Teresa Rejadell provided a valuable commentary on discerning God's will. Sister Teresa's community was undergoing a stressful period of transition, and she had become deeply anxious. She appealed to Ignatius for guidance. He wrote an extended letter in response, describing ways of seeing God's will for her. The following are some excerpts from this extraordinary letter, dated June 18, 1536:

May the grace and love of Christ our Lord be our never-failing protection. . . .

I will call your attention briefly to two lessons which our Lord usually gives, or permits. The one of them He gives, the other

55

He permits. The first is an interior consolation which casts out all uneasiness and draws one to a complete love of our Lord. . . . When this divine consolation is present all trials are pleasant and all weariness rest. . . . This consolation points out and opens up the way we are to follow and points out the way we are to avoid. . . .

But when this consolation is absent the other lesson comes to light. Our ancient enemy sets up all possible obstacles to turn us aside from the way on which we have entered. He makes use of everything to vex us, and everything in the first lesson is reversed. We find ourselves sad without knowing why. We cannot pray with devotion, nor contemplate, nor even speak or hear of the things of God with any interior taste or relish. Not only this, but if he sees that we are weak and much humbled by these harmful thoughts, he goes on to suggest that we are entirely forgotten by God our Lord, and leads us to think that we are quite separated from Him and that all that we have done and all that we desire to do is entirely worthless. He thus endeavors to bring us to a state of general discouragement. We can thus see what causes our fear and weakness: it is a too-prolonged gaze at such times on our miseries. We allow ourselves to be laid low by his misleading suggestions. For this reason it is necessary for us to be aware of our opponent. If we are in consolation, we should abase and humble ourselves and reflect that soon the trial of temptation will come. And when temptation, darkness, or sadness comes upon us, we must go contrary to it without permitting ourselves to pay any attention to the unpleasant impressions caused in us, and hope patiently for the consolation of our Lord, which will cast out all our uneasiness and scatter all the clouds. . . . In closing I beg the most holy Trinity to bestow upon us all plentiful grace to know God's most holy will and perfectly to fulfill it. (*Letters*, 8, 21–24)

Pause: Consider a recent experience in which you felt interiorly pulled between two opposing forces.

Ignatius's Words

In his Spiritual Exercises, Ignatius outlined two ways of making a good "election," or choice. These rules describe the second way:

First Rule. The love which moves and causes one to choose must come from above, that is, from the love of God, so that the one who is making the decision first feels that the greater or lesser attraction to the object of choice is actually love for the Creator and Lord.

Second Rule. I should imagine a person whom I have never seen or known, and whom I would like to see practice all perfection. Then I should consider what I would tell that person to do and choose for the greater glory of God. . . . Then I will do the same, myself keeping the rule I have proposed for another.

Third Rule. This is to consider what procedure and norm of action I would wish to have followed in making the present election if I were at the moment of death. . . .

Fourth Rule. I should picture and reflect on myself standing in the presence of my Judge on the last day, and consider what election in the present matter I would then wish to have made. I will now choose that rule of life that I would then wish to have observed, that on the day of judgment I may be filled with happiness and joy.

—*Spiritual Exercises*, 60–61

Reflection

For Ignatius, "life is a battleground, and the stakes are enormous. . . . The prizes of the battle are the hearts and minds of human beings" (William A. Barry, "Ignatius of Loyola's Discernment of Spirits").

Each of us can identify with this statement; our tents also are pitched on that battleground. At times, we are thrown into confusion as we try to sort out our feelings, promptings, and desires in the decisions we face each day. We vacillate in an inner dialogue that can be paralyzing: "What should I do?" "What do I want?" "What does God want of me?" "What if I fail?" The questions swirl like a tornado.

In his letter to Sister Teresa, Ignatius encouraged her, and us, to examine the promptings experienced within and to be sensitive to whether they are of the Spirit of God or from a spirit of darkness and evil. Ignatius reminded us that it is not always easy to tell the difference. He taught us that if we are to grow in wholeness and freedom, it is essential that we discern the movements of the Spirit.

So important was discernment to Ignatius that he insisted that the companions make a daily examen of consciousness. What a retreat is to a year, and what prayer is to a day, the examen is to the moment-by-moment discernment of God's Spirit in the circumstances and events of everyday life.

▶ Read the excerpts from Ignatius's letter to Sister Teresa in "About Ignatius" again. When you find a passage that strikes you as important to you, spend time meditating on it. Slowly read the passage over and over. Let its meaning for you become apparent.

▶ Read "Ignatius's Words" again. Then reflect on these questions:

- Would these rules of Ignatius's be helpful in my making a decision right now?
- Would my life have more focus and meaning if I discerned important decisions with a method like the one developed by Ignatius?
- Would receiving spiritual direction be helpful in discerning the movements of God's Spirit in my life?

▶ Recall three major decisions you have made in the past. For each one, consider your feelings as you remember the issues, the choices, the struggles, the decision, and the decision's effects. What do your reflections tell you about the pattern of the Spirit's movement within you? How can this be helpful to you for the future?

▶ Using the following prayer based on the suggestions of Ignatius, make your own daily examen of consciousness:

God, my creator, I am totally dependent on you. Everything is a gift from you. All is a gift. I give you thanks and praise for the gifts of this day.

Holy Spirit, I believe you work through and in time to reveal me to myself. Please give me an increased awareness of how you are guiding and shaping my life, as well as a more sensitive awareness of the obstacles I put in your way.

You have been present in my life today. Be near, now, as I reflect on these things:

- your presence in the events of today
- your presence in the feelings I experienced today
- your call to me
- my response to you

God, I ask your loving forgiveness and healing. The particular event of this day that I most want healed is _____.

Filled with hope and a firm belief in your love and power, I entrust myself to your care and strongly affirm _____ [claim the gift you most desire, most need; believe that God desires to give you that gift].

From God's Word

Beloved, do not believe every spirit, but test the spirits to see whether they are from God; for many false prophets have gone out into the world. By this you know the Spirit of God: every spirit that confesses that Jesus Christ has come in the flesh is from God, and every spirit that does not confess Jesus is not from God. And this is the spirit of the antichrist, of which you have heard that it is coming; and now it is already in the world.

—1 John 4:1–3

Closing prayer: "Give me, O Christ, the courage of faith. Pierce the hidden depths of my spirit like a two-edged sword. Give me your clear light to guide my conscience. Give me that love which delights me in the seclusion of my timid heart and without which I cannot know you as the Lord of all things, of atoms and stars, of human bodies and spiritual worlds. Then shall I be truly blessed in you, then shall I have my heart's desire and the purpose of my existence."

—Prayer of Hugo Rahner, in *The New Book of Christian Prayers*, 40

Living in God's Presence

Theme: Ignatius affirmed all of creation, seeing in all things the presence of God.

Opening prayer: Gracious God, your presence permeates all of creation, which is alive with your love. You smile in the hearts of your children. Open our eyes to see your brightness everywhere and always.

About Ignatius

While Ignatius was still at Manresa, he had an experience on the banks of the river Cardoner that proved to be a decisive moment in his life:

> He was going out of his devotion to a church a little more than a mile from Manresa; I believe it was called St. Paul's. The road ran next to the river. As he went along occupied with his devotions, he sat down for a little while with his face toward the river which was running deep. While he was seated there, the eyes of his understanding began to be opened; though he did not see any vision, he understood and knew many things, both spiritual things and matters of faith and of learning, and this was with so great an enlightenment that everything seemed new to him. Though there were many, he cannot set forth the details that he understood then, except that he experienced a great clarity in his understanding. This was such that in the whole course of his

life, through sixty-two years, even if he gathered up all the many helps he had had from God and all the many things he knew and added them together, he does not think they would amount to as much as he had received at that one time. (*Autobiography,* 39–40)

Pause: Remember a time when you received a totally surprising, pure gift of God's presence.

Ignatius's Words

Ignatius's profound experience of God's presence is exemplified in the following excerpt from one of his letters. Father Brandao had submitted a list of sixteen questions regarding the spiritual life and practices of the men who were living in the Jesuit houses of study. Ignatius responded:

Considering the end of our studies, the scholastics can hardly give themselves to prolonged meditations. Over and above the spiritual exercises assigned for their perfection—namely, daily Mass, an hour for vocal prayer and examen of conscience, and weekly confession and Communion—they should practice the seeking of God's presence in all things, in their conversations, their walks, in all that they see, taste, hear, understand, in all their actions, since His Divine Majesty is truly in all things by His presence, power, and essence. This kind of meditation, which finds God our Lord in all things, is easier than raising oneself to the consideration of divine truths which are more abstract and which demand something of an effort if we are to keep our attention on them. But this method is an excellent exercise to prepare us for great visitations of our Lord, even in prayers that are rather short. Besides this, the scholastics can frequently offer to God our Lord their studies and the efforts they demand, seeing that they have undertaken them for His love.

—*Letters*, 240

Reflection

Ignatius experienced God's presence by the river, in study, while celebrating the liturgy, in service to poor people, in conversations, at meals—everywhere. This sense of God's presence consoled and supported him. Simple awareness of God's presence becomes a prayer, like the comfortable communication of care experienced in the silence between two friends.

The spirit of Ignatius's keen sense of God's presence in all of life can be seen in the poetry of Jesuit Gerard Manley Hopkins, who proclaimed:

The world is charged with the grandeur of God.
   It will flame out, like shining from shook foil;
   It gathers to a greatness, like the ooze of oil
Crushed. Why do men then now not reck his rod?
Generations have trod, have trod, have trod;
   And all is seared with trade; bleared, smeared with toil;
   And wears man's smudge and shares man's smell: the soil
Is bare now, nor can foot feel, being shod.
And for all this, nature is never spent;
   There lives the dearest freshness deep down things;
And though the last lights off the black West went
   Oh, morning, at the brown brink eastward, springs—
Because the Holy Ghost over the bent

World broods with warm breast and with ah! bright wings.

—"God's Grandeur," *Poems and Prose of*
Gerard Manley Hopkins, 27

The world is "charged with the grandeur of God" if we can but
see it.

▶ Go for a stroll on the banks of a river or stream, in a forest clearing, under a starlit sky, or to some other favorite spot in nature.
Take your time. Allow yourself to see, touch, smell, hear, and even
taste all the goodness abounding there. Enter into your experience with intention. And as you feel the prompting of your spirit,
respond to the Creator.

▶ In the Fourth Week of the Spiritual Exercises, Ignatius invites
us to "The Contemplation to Gain Love." The steps in this meditation are paraphrased here. Before you begin, relax. Breathe deeply
and slowly, allowing God's Spirit to fill your heart.

- Remember that God is present around and within you.
  Invite God into conversation.
- Ask God to enlighten your understanding and appreciation
  of all the wonders you have been given in creation.
- Recall that God has given you everything that is good as a
  free gift. Bring to mind all the gifts you have been given.
- Express your love and thanks to God for all of God's gifts by
  offering Ignatius's prayer, as follows:

Take, Lord, and receive all my liberty, my memory, my understanding, and my entire will, all that I have and possess. You have
given all to me. To you, Lord, I return it. All is yours. Dispose
of it wholly according to your will. Give me your love and your
grace. That is enough for me. (*Spiritual Exercises*, 79)

- Bring to consciousness these gifts from God's bounty to you: your dearest friends, beloved family members, blessed events, important insights, scenes from nature's grandeur. Let your consciousness relish each memory or experience. Respond by praying, "Take, Lord, and receive."
- Recall that God sent Jesus to show us the loving face of God. God loves us so completely that the Holy Spirit dwells within our very souls. We are created in God's image. Pray, "Take, Lord, and receive."
- Consider that God loves us unconditionally. God's love showers down on us like life-giving sunlight or the nourishing rain. God calls us to full life. Offer the prayer "Take, Lord, and receive."
- End this reflection by slowly praying the Lord's Prayer.

▶ Consider ways in which you can bring yourself into God's presence throughout your day.

From God's Word

O God, our God,
how glorious is your name over all the earth!
Your glory is praised in the heavens.
Out of the mouths of children and babes
you have fashioned praise. . . .
When I look at your heavens, the work of your hands,
the moon and the stars which you created—
who are we that you should be mindful of us,
that you should care for us?
You have made us little less than the gods
and crowned us with glory and honor.

God, our God,
how glorious is your name over all the earth!

—Psalm 8, *Psalms Anew*

Closing prayer:

Glory be to God for dappled things—
  For skies of couple-colour as a brinded cow;
    For rose-moles all in stipple upon trout that swim;
Fresh-firecoal chestnut-falls; finches' wings;
Landscape plotted and pieced—fold, fallow, and plough;
  And áll trádes, their gear and tackle and trim.
All things counter, original, spare, strange;
Whatever is fickle, freckled (who knows how?)
  With swift, slow; sweet, sour; adazzle, dim;
He fathers-forth whose beauty is past change:
  Praise him.

—"Pied Beauty," Hopkins, *Poems and Prose*, 30–31

Loving Service

Theme: In the midst of loving service, Ignatius experienced God. Like all Christians, Ignatius was called to be a contemplative in action.

Opening prayer: "[Gracious God,] how am I to set about showing you and proving to myself, through some external effort, that I am not one of those who say Lord, Lord! with their lips only? . . . I shall respond by taking great care never to stifle nor distort nor waste my power to love and to do."

—de Chardin, *Divine Milieu*, 79

About Ignatius

While the mystical experience at La Storta confirmed in Ignatius his identity and union with Christ, it simultaneously called him to service. One of Ignatius's first companions, Diego Laynez, provided this explanation:

> Jesus with the cross on his shoulders appeared to Ignatius, and by His side the Father, who said to Him: "I desire you to take this man for your servant." Jesus then turned to Ignatius and said to him, "It is my will that you serve Us." The pronoun in the plural, Us, imparts to this vision a seal clearly trinitarian. The Father unites Ignatius closely with Jesus bearing the cross, and expresses His will that Ignatius should dedicate himself to their service. Ignatius is called to a mysticism of union, to be "placed

with Christ," and also of service, by being invited to consecrate his life to the divine service. (*Ignatius of Loyola*, 153)

The end result of his God-given natural character and temperament, his infused contemplation, his university studies, and his experiences in founding and organizing the Society was a mysticism which impelled him not merely toward love of God in contemplative solitude but also toward service through love. Intense union with God within the soul was combined with a powerful orientation toward apostolic activity. . . . His ideal of apostolic spirituality was to seek and find God in all things. (*Constitutions*, 22–23)

In Alcalá and Salamanca, Ignatius preached, taught religion, and tended sick people. In Paris, he gave the fruits of his own begging to people more needy than himself. In Venice, he and his companions labored in charity hospitals. When he arrived in Rome, Ignatius continued to serve God's people. During the famine of 1538–1539, he and the Jesuits sheltered hundreds of homeless people. He opened the home of St. Martha to protect and reeducate some of Rome's prostitutes. To protect young girls from being exploited, he founded the orphanage of Santa Maria. Meanwhile, he preached throughout the city and directed the Spiritual Exercises for people seeking to reform their lives.

Pause: How is the service that you render to other people a meeting place with God?

Ignatius's Words

In a letter to Peter Canisius, who had recently been ordained, Ignatius wrote these words of encouragement:

Study and ponder the vocation to which you have been called. Make use of the grace which in Christ has been given you . . . never resist it. The same Lord it is who worketh in us both to will and to accomplish, according to His good will, which is in itself infinite and all-glorious and ineffable for us through Christ Jesus. For the Spirit of Jesus will give thee in all things understanding and fortitude, to the end that through you the name of Jesus will be glorified and bear much fruit in many souls, with the hope of a better life.

I write this to you with the idea of giving spurs to the willing horse, as the proverb goes. For the rest, you have won all our love in the Lord by your fearless activity in the Lord's vineyard and have led me to form the great hope that Jesus Christ will be glorified in you right to the end.

—Letters, 97

Reflection

Even though we struggle to integrate our prayer life into our daily routine, Jesus clearly called us to compassionate service, especially for the people most in need. Melding our "being" with our "doing" proves a constant challenge. Ignatius reached a balance of prayer and action, realizing that one without the other puts our spirituality out of harmony.

Pedro Arrupe, former superior general of the Jesuits, remarked:

Service is the key idea of the charism of Ignatius. It is an idea whose moving power achieved in the life and spirituality of Ignatius—even in his mystical phase—a total realization: unconditioned and limitless service, service that is large-hearted and humble. It could be said that even the Trinitarian "lights," which enriched his mystical life, rather than leading to a passive and contemplative quieting, spurred him to a greater service of this God he contemplated with such great love and reverence. (*Challenge*, 254)

Ignatius called us to be contemplatives in action. Only by being radically centered in Christ can we find the energy that will transform itself into loving, creative, and healing service.

▶ Reflect on the rhythm of your life during the past week. Trace the cycle of action, prayer, and action during these seven days of your life. How has your prayer influenced your action? How have your activities affected you and brought you to prayer?

▶ Ponder these questions about the balance between prayer and service in your life:

- How does a consistent, disciplined life of prayer enable you to carry the message of your Christian beliefs and values to others, and to practice these principles in all your affairs?

- How content are you with your prayer? Are you being called to make some changes?

▶ In Ignatian spirituality, self-forgetful love provides the foundation for service. We learn self-sacrifice, charity, compassion, empathy, and love from the example of other people. Who in your life exemplifies self-forgetful loving? Remember and thank God for their presence in your life.

▶ Today, do your work with special care and attentive kindness to others. Several times during the day, stop a few moments and ponder these questions:

- How is my work itself of service to God's people?

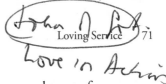

- How is the manner in which I do my work part of my service to other people?

- How can I make my work and the way I do it an act of prayer through service?

▶ Converse with Jesus about your life of service, asking for the grace you need to be generous and compassionate in service to your sisters and brothers.

▶ Today, act with special kindness toward someone you find difficult.

From God's Word

Jesus told his followers that when they stood before the throne of justice, he would tell those invited into glory, "I was hungry and you gave me food; I was thirsty and you gave me drink; I was a stranger and you made me welcome; naked and you clothed me, sick and you visited me, in prison and you came to see me." Then the virtuous will say to him in reply, "When did we see you hungry and feed you, or thirsty and give you drink? When did we see you a stranger and make you welcome, naked and clothe you, sick or in prison and go to see you?" And Jesus will answer, "I tell you solemnly, in so far as you did this to one of the least of these brothers and sisters of mine, you did it to me."

—Adapted from Matthew 25:31–40

Closing prayer: "[Loving God,] with that voice that you make groan in the depths of my being I seek the copious pouring out of Yourself, like the rain that gives back life to the arid earth, and like a breath of life that comes to animate dry bones. Give me that Spirit that scrutinizes all, inspires all, teaches all, that will strengthen me to support what I am not able to support. Give me that Spirit that transformed the weak Galilean fishermen into the columns of your Church and into Apostles who gave in the holocaust of their lives the supreme testimony of their love for their brothers [and sisters]."

—*Challenge*, 296–297

Meditation 12

Love for the Church

Theme: Ignatius had a profound love for and sense of the church as the body of Christ. Never naive about the frailty of its leaders, he remained a faithful and true son of the church, working diligently for its renewal in the spirit of the gospel.

Opening prayer: Jesus, Good Shepherd, thank you for the great gift of your church. Place us at its heart and keep us faithful to its vision.

About Ignatius

During his vision at La Storta, Ignatius heard the words *Ego ero vobis Romae propitius*, or "I will be propitious to you in Rome" (*Placed with Jesus*, 385):

> These words explicated the ecclesial dimension of the companions' service of Christ carrying his Cross, which was confirmed and focused in the person of the Roman pontiff, the Vicar of Christ on earth. Jerusalem, where Ignatius and his companions had hoped to go, laboring for the good of souls in the same villages and towns in which Christ has preached and suffered—this Jerusalem, at La Storta, took the shape of Rome. One year later, in November of 1538, the companions offered themselves to the Pope and shortly thereafter institutionalized their "Society of Jesus" as a religious order, which has the vow and promise to God

of obedience to the Vicar of Christ as "its first principle and most basic foundation."

As Polanco, Ignatius's secretary, said of the early companions, "They were all convinced that Christ himself, through the mediation of his Vicar, would vouchsafe to show them the way to his greater service." (*Placed with Jesus*, 385–386, 392)

Pause: How would you describe your relationship with the church?

Ignatius's Words

In a time when the institutional church operated far from the ideal of the gospel, Ignatius cherished a deep love for Sancta Mater Ecclesia, *Holy Mother Church. It was a broken church, burdened with human frailty and the effects of the confusion and turmoil of the sixteenth century.*

Ignatius proposed eighteen guidelines to help people maintain balance and clear judgment during a period of change and renewal in the church. A contemporary paraphrase of the rules for fostering the "True Sentiment Which We Ought to Have in the Church Militant" reveals their lasting value:

1. When legitimate authority speaks within the Church, we should listen with receptive ears and be more prompt to respond favorably than to criticize in a condemnatory way. . . .

9. The law and precepts within the Church are meant to be of help for the institutional life of the Body of Christ. As a result, we should maintain a proper respect for such laws

and respond with all our heart to them for the good order of the whole Body.

10. We should be more ready to give our support and approval to our leaders, both in their personal conduct and in their directives, than to find fault with them. Only greater dissatisfaction and disunity among us is caused by public criticism and defamation of character. Rather the proper step in remedying a wrong, harmful, unjust, or scandalous situation would be to refer and make representation to the persons who can do something about the problem. . . .

14. It will always remain difficult to describe adequately the saving will of God. That God wants all people to be saved is revealed. That [people have] the freedom to reject God in a decisive way is also our belief. We should be careful in our thinking and speaking about this matter not to begin to deny either of these two essential statements of our Christian faith. . . .

18. Today we have a great emphasis on the motivation of love being central to our Christian lives. Yet we can so overstress a language of love, that we ignore the value of Christian fear—the fear . . . which acknowledges God as God and the filial fear of offending a [parent] who loves us. And so in the practical living of our Christian lives, we must acknowledge and make use of the various motivating factors which stimulate us towards growth and development in Christ.

—Fleming, *Spiritual Exercises*, 281–291

Reflection

Today, as in the time of Ignatius, the church often appears to be a tangled web of misery and majesty. Perhaps the proof of the divine mission of the church is that it survives the human frailty of its members. The church continues to be a light to the nations, a herald of truth, and a sign of hope and unity. The renowned Jesuit theologian Karl Rahner tried to imagine what Ignatius would tell his companions now about the church. Assuming the voice of Ignatius, Rahner said:

> I loved the Church as the realization of God's love for the physical body of his son in history. In this mystical union of God with the Church—in spite of the radical difference between them—the Church itself was and remained a way to God for me and the point of my inexpressible relationship to the eternal mystery. . . .
>
> There is no principle in the Church which says that the convictions and decisions of Christians and office-holders should automatically integrate without friction. The Church is a Church of the spirit of the infinite and incomprehensible God, whose perfect unity can only be mirrored in this world in many different facets. The Church's final perfected unity is God . . . and nothing else. (*Ignatius*, 27–28)

Despite conflicts and developments in the church, it remains an essential point of contact with God's will and goodness.

▶ The church needs our love and faithfulness. After reviewing the history of the sinfulness of the church, Henri de Lubac, SJ, a spiritual son of Ignatius, asked the question, "How can I encompass and understand this church?" His answer was, "The church is my mother" ("Meditation on the Church," in *Vatican II: An Interfaith Appraisal*, 260).

- In your own experience, have you seen the church as having sinned? If so, how?

- How do you feel about de Lubac's response? Can you love the church like a mother?

▶ Ponder each of these questions:

- How does the church continue to be a light to the nations?
- Where is the church a herald of truth?
- How is the church a sign of hope and unity?
- In what ways is the church a servant to humankind's physical, intellectual, or psychological needs?

▶ What is your picture of the ideal church? What responsibility are you assuming for its realization?

▶ Consider what you would say about your experience of the church to a complete stranger who is unfamiliar with it. What things would you tend to stress about the church?

▶ Compose your own prayer for the church, for any healing that you need in your relationship with the church, and for any renewal the church needs to undertake.

From God's Word

Now when Jesus came into the district of Caesarea Philippi, he asked his disciples, "Who do people say that the Son of Man is?" And they said, "Some say John the Baptist, but others Elijah, and still others Jeremiah or one of the prophets." He said to them, "But who do you say that I am?" Simon Peter answered, "You are the Messiah, the Son of the living God." And Jesus answered him, "Blessed are you, Simon son of Jonah! For flesh and blood has not revealed this to you, but my Father in heaven. And I tell you, you are

Peter, and on this rock I will build my church, and the gates of Hades will not prevail against it. I will give you the keys of . . . heaven, and whatever you bind on earth will be bound in heaven, and whatever you loose on earth will be loosed in heaven."

—Matthew 16:13–19

Closing prayer: Loving God, giver of all good gifts, by the power of the risen Christ, give your church strength to overcome, in patience and love, sorrow and difficulties, both those that are from within and those that are from without. May your church ever reveal in the world, faithfully, however darkly, the mystery of God until the time when it shall be manifested in full light.

—Adapted from "Lumen Gentium,"
in *Documents of Vatican II*, 358

Meditation 13

Sustained by the Bread of Life

Theme: From the Eucharist, Ignatius drew daily sustenance for his preeminently active ministry.

Opening prayer: Gracious God, in the Eucharist, you have given us your Son, the source of life. Deepen in us an appreciation of the meal you place before us daily. May it be for us, as it was for Ignatius, bread for the way.

About Ignatius

In his autobiography, Ignatius described an experience of the Eucharist during his time at Manresa.

> One day in this town while [Ignatius] was hearing mass in the church of the monastery . . . at the elevation of the Body of the Lord, he saw with interior eyes something like white rays coming from above. Although he cannot explain this very well after so long a time, nevertheless what he saw clearly with his understanding was how Jesus Christ our Lord was there in that most holy sacrament. (*Autobiography*, 38)

One of his biographers made these remarks:

> It is the Mass of each day which forms the clearly apparent center of the graces noted down for the rest of the day. His awakening and his rising with the thought of the Mass in his mind, his prayer and his interior preparation for the Holy Sacrifice,

his preparing the altar and the vestments, the beginning of the
Mass and its different parts, and his thanksgiving—such are the
moments to which are related the vast majority of the favors he
records. Even those which were received during the course of the
day always seem like a prolonging or a complement of those of
the morning. (de Guibert, *Jesuits*, 53)

Pause: Recall your most recent Eucharist. How was it a gift for
your day?

Ignatius's Words

*In his journal, Ignatius repeatedly related the extraordinary
infusion of grace that accompanied his celebration of the
Eucharist. This selection refers to a discernment he made
regarding poverty for the society:*

While preparing the altar, the thought of Jesus occurring to
me, I felt a movement to follow Him. . . .

I went along with these thoughts and vested while they
increased, and took them as a confirmation, although I
received no consolations on this point, and thinking that
the appearance of Jesus was in some way from the Most
Holy Trinity, I recalled the day when the Father placed me
with the Son. As I finished vesting with this intention of
impressing on my mind the name of Jesus, and trying to
think that a confirmation for the future, a fresh attack of tears
and sobbing came upon me, as I began Mass helped with
much grace and devotion, and with quiet tears for the most
part, and even when I had finished, the great devotion and
movement to tears lasted until I had unvested.

Throughout the Mass, I had various feelings in confirmation
of what I had said, and, as I held the Blessed Sacrament in

my hands, the word came to me with an intense interior movement never to leave Him for all heaven and earth, etc., while I felt fresh movements of devotion and spiritual joy. . . . Later in the day, as often as I thought of Jesus, or remembered Him, I had a certain feeling, or saw with my understanding, with a continuous and confirming devotion.

—*Spiritual Journal*, 15–16

Reflection

The tears of Ignatius were an outward sign of the intensity of his interior devotion and the central place the Eucharist held for him in daily life.

His example invites us to reflect on our own understanding of and devotion to the Eucharist, which is, as Vatican Council II reminded us, "a sacrament of love, a sign of unity, a bond of charity, a paschal banquet in which Christ is consumed, the mind is filled with grace, and a pledge of future glory is given to us" (Flannery, *Documents*, 16).

▶ Reflect on the passage from Vatican Council II. Then, meditate on these questions:

- How is the Eucharist a sacrament of love for me?
- Does the Eucharist become my pledge of unity with my family, my friends, my local community, my parish, and the global family?
- Do I commit myself to a bond of charity when I partake of the Eucharist?

Ask God for the gift of a deepening love for the Eucharist.

▶ Remember your First Communion. Recall it in detail: your preparation for it, the kind of day it was, how you dressed, the Mass, your feelings and prayer, and any celebration that followed.

▶ When you next receive the Eucharist, pray the following litany composed of a partial list of all the names and titles Ignatius used in his writings when speaking of or to Jesus:

> Jesus, Son of the Virgin, Have mercy on us.
> Jesus, our Creator and Lord,
> Jesus, eternal Lord of all things,
> Jesus, who created and redeemed us,
> Jesus, who is to be our eternal judge,
> Jesus, divine majesty,
> Jesus, complete and perfect goodness,
> Jesus, infinite love,
> Jesus, our kindly Lord,
> Jesus, infinite wisdom,
> Jesus, author and source of every blessing,
> Jesus, the giver of every gift,
> Jesus, our perfect and eternal good,
> Jesus, our salvation,
> Jesus, our help and support,
> Jesus, our Mediator,
> Jesus, the power of God,
> Jesus, our supreme leader and Lord,
> Jesus, our food and companion in pilgrimage,
> Jesus, beautiful and lovable,
> Jesus, poor and humble,
> Jesus, our consoler,
> Jesus, our peace,
> Jesus, our joy,

Jesus, our hope,

Jesus, our life,

Jesus, our reward exceedingly great,

Jesus, true life of the world,

Jesus, our model and guide,

Jesus, the head of your body the Church,

Jesus, the bridegroom of the Church your Spouse,

Jesus, your Father has placed us with you,

Jesus, we have cast the anchor of our hope in you,

Jesus, make us conform to the will of the most Holy Trinity,

Jesus, be the means of our union with the most Holy Trinity,

—Blessed be the name of Jesus, who provides for us in so many

ways. . . . Amen.

—*Ever to Love and to Serve: Prayer Services on*
Ignatian Themes, 1–2

From God's Word

I tell you most solemnly,
Moses did not give you bread from heaven,
God gives you the bread from heaven,
the true bread;
for God's bread
comes down from heaven
and gives life to the world.
I am the bread of life.
Anyone who comes to me will never be hungry;
anyone who believes in me will never be thirsty.

—Adapted from John

Closing prayer: "Grant, O God, that when I draw near to the altar to communicate, I may henceforth discern the infinite perspectives hidden beneath the smallness and the nearness of the Host in which you are concealed. I have already accustomed myself to seeing, beneath the stillness of that piece of bread, a devouring power which, in the words of the greatest doctors of your Church, far from being consumed by me, consumes me. Give me the strength to rise above the remaining illusions which tend to make me think of your touch as circumscribed and momentary."

—*Divine Milieu*, 126

Mary, Our Mother

Theme: From his early years, Ignatius had a sense of Mary's presence. His writings present Mary as the one who conducts him into the presence of the Trinity.

Opening prayer: "God, you gave the Virgin Mary a share in the passion of your Son and in the glory of his resurrection. Turn our eyes to look on [Christ] so that we may seek [the reign of God] on earth and enter into everlasting life, to be one with Mary, our Mother. We ask this through Christ. . . ."
—"Prayer over the Gifts," in *Supplement to the Missal and Lectionary for the Society of Jesus,* 15

About Ignatius

As a young man, Ignatius dreamed of a woman for whom he would do anything. He wrote in his autobiography:

Of the many vain things that presented themselves to him, one took such a hold on his heart that he was absorbed in thinking about it for two or three or four hours without realizing it: he imagined what he would do in the service of a certain lady, the means he would take so he could go to the country where she lived, the verses, the words he would say to her, the deeds of arms he would do in her service. He became so conceited with this that he did not consider how impossible it would be because the lady was not of the lower nobility nor a countess nor a duchess, but her station was higher than any of these.

Nevertheless, Our Lord assisted him, causing other thoughts that arose from the things he read to follow these. . . .

And so he began to forget the thoughts of the past with these holy desires he had, and they were confirmed by a vision in this manner. One night while he was awake, he saw clearly an image of Our Lady with the holy child Jesus. (*Autobiography*, 23–24)

In light of his vision of Mary, Ignatius made pilgrimages to the shrines of Mary. He dedicated himself to praying the Office of Our Lady. At Montserrat, on the feast of the Annunciation, he surrendered his sword and dagger, placing them at Mary's feet.

Ignatius, who had dreamed of a lady for whom he would do anything, found in Mary the lady who would be for him the doorway of the graces he would receive throughout his life. He asked Mary to grant his greatest desire, "to deign to place him with her Son" (*Autobiography*, 89).

Pause: Consider the picture or image of Mary that you most enjoy.

Ignatius's Words

In his spiritual journal, Ignatius made frequent references to Mary, giving expression to a strong and tender relationship with her and to the great gift of her presence in his life. He made this entry on February 15, 1544:

Later, on going out to say Mass, when beginning the prayer, I saw a likeness of our Lady, and realized how serious had been my fault of the other day, not without some interior movement and tears, thinking that the Blessed Virgin felt ashamed at asking for me so often after my many failings, so much so, that our Lady hid herself from me, and I found no devotion either in her or from on high. After this, as I did not find our Lady, I sought comfort on high, and there came upon me a great movement of tears and sobbing with a certain assurance that the Heavenly Father was showing Himself favorable and kindly, so much so, that He gave me a sign that it would be pleasing to Him to be asked through our Lady, whom I could not see.

While preparing the altar, and after vesting, and during the Mass, very intense interior movements, and many and intense tears and sobbing, with frequent loss of speech, and also after the end of Mass, and for long periods during the Mass, preparing and afterwards, the clear view of our Lady, very propitious before the Father, to such an extent, that in the prayers to the Father, to the Son, and at the consecration, I could not help feeling and seeing her, as though she were a part, or the doorway, of all the grace I felt in my soul. At the consecration she showed that her flesh was in that of her Son, with such great light that I cannot write about it.

—*Spiritual Journal*, 7

Reflection

Throughout history, devotion to Mary has served as a remedy for the harsh, rigid, or decadent times in the church. In 1950, the psychologist Carl Jung hailed the proclamation of the dogma of the assumption of Mary. On several occasions, Jung publicly declared that the world needed the sign of the woman who was assumed into heaven, body as well as soul, as an antidote for the materialism of our time (Carl G. Jung, *Four Archetypes: Mother, Rebirth, Spirit, Trickster*, 41–43).

An authentic devotion to Mary has always effected a powerful transformation in the life of Christians. On the spiritual journey, Mary models full humanity: she was strong and tender, challenging and nurturing, active and contemplative. She courageously welcomed her motherhood. She stood at the crucifixion, whereas the apostles denied Jesus.

God calls all of us to be holy and to be wholly human, and so we are invited to put aside stereotypes of masculinity and femininity and to put on our full humanity, as did Mary and Jesus. Ignatian spirituality challenges us to offer our total humanity to the service of God's reign, just as Mary did, and to depend on her loving intercession.

▶ At the Annunciation, Mary displayed complete trust in God and surrendered to God's will. God showers us with grace so that we too can trust God's goodness; act courageously for love, peace, and justice; and surrender to God's will.

- In what areas of your life do you need to trust more completely in God's goodness?
- In dealing with which situations do you need more courage to love, make peace, and act justly?
- What aspects of your life do you need to surrender to God's will, to let go of and let God take care of?
- In your journal or on a piece of paper, converse with Mary about each of these questions. Proceed with this conversation, first one speaking, then the other—for example:

You: Blessed Mother, I just cannot trust that . . .
Mary: [Her response to you]

▶ In the Spiritual Exercises, Ignatius describes three methods of prayer. The third method is this:

> With each breath or respiration, one should pray mentally while saying a single word of the Lord's Prayer, or of another prayer, in such a way that from one breath to another, only one word is said. During this period of time, the attention should be directed primarily to the meaning of the word, to the Person who is addressed. . . . In this way, observing the same measure of time, one should go through the remaining words of the prayer. (*Spiritual Exercises*, 84)

Using this Ignatian method of prayer, pray the Hail Mary:

> Hail Mary, full of grace,
> the Lord is with you.
> Blessed are you among women,
> and blessed is the fruit of your womb, Jesus.
> Holy Mary, mother of God,
> Pray for us sinners,
> now and at the hour of our death. Amen.

▶ Picture yourself as John, standing at the foot of the cross. Look up and see Jesus dying. He looks at Mary and at you and says, "Woman, here is your son. . . . [Son,] here is your mother" (John 19:26–27). Standing there, you reflect on his words, pondering these questions:

- How will you take Mary into your home?
- How will you welcome her into your heart?

After meditating on these questions, tell Mary what is in your heart.

▶ Relishing each word, phrase, and image, read aloud this poem to
Mary, written by Gerard Manley Hopkins and titled "The Blessed
Virgin Compared to the Air We Breathe":

Wild air, world-mothering air,
Nestling me everywhere,
That each eyelash or hair
Girdles; goes home betwixt
The fleeciest, frailest-flixed
Snowflake; that's fairly mixed
With, riddles, and is rife
In every least thing's life;
This needful, never spent,
And nursing element;
My more than meat and drink,
My meal at every wink;
This air, which, by life's law,
My lung must draw and draw
Now but to breathe its praise,
Minds me in many ways
Of her who not only
Gave God's infinity
Dwindled to infancy
Welcome in womb and breast,
Birth, milk, and all the rest
But mothers each new grace
That does now reach our race—
Mary Immaculate,
Merely a woman, yet
Whose presence, power is
Great as no goddess's

Was deemèd, dreamèd; who
This one work has to do—
Let all God's glory through,
God's glory which would go
Through her and from her flow
Off, and no way but so. . . .

—Hopkins, *Poems and Prose*, 54–55

▶ Sing your favorite hymn to Mary.

From God's Word

In those days Mary set out and went with haste to a Judean town in the hill country, where she entered the house of Zechariah and greeted Elizabeth. When Elizabeth heard Mary's greeting, the child leapt in her womb. And Elizabeth was filled with the Holy Spirit and exclaimed with a loud cry, "Blessed are you among women, and blessed is the fruit of your womb. And why has this happened to me, that the mother of my Lord comes to me? For as soon as I heard the sound of your greeting, the child in my womb leapt for joy. And blessed is she who believed that there would be a fulfilment of what was spoken to her by the Lord."

—Luke 1:39–45

Closing prayer: Mary, Mother of Jesus, place me with your Son.

The Triune God

Theme: Ignatius had a great devotion to the blessed Trinity. He prayed daily to each of the persons, and references to this greatest of all mysteries fill his writings.

Opening prayer: "Great God of my life, I will praise Thee on the three shores of Thy one light."

—"Te Deum," in Gertrude von Le Fort, *Hymns to the Church*, 51

About Ignatius

Using the image of three notes or keys producing a single harmony, Ignatius described the moment of grace that sealed his devotion to the Trinity:

[Ignatius] had great devotion to the Most Holy Trinity, and each day he said a prayer to the three Persons individually. But as he also said a prayer to the Most Holy Trinity the thought came to him: why did he say four prayers to the Trinity? But this thought, as something of small importance, gave him little or no difficulty. One day while saying the Hours of Our Lady on the steps of the monastery itself, his understanding began to be elevated so that he saw the Most Holy Trinity in the form of three keys. This brought on so many tears and so much sobbing that he could not control himself. While going in a procession that set out from there that morning, he could not hold back his tears until dinnertime; after eating he could not stop talking about the Most Holy Trinity, using many different comparisons and with great joy and consolation. As a result the impression of experiencing great devotion while praying to the Most Holy Trinity has remained with him throughout his life. (*Autobiography*, 37–38)

Pause: Slowly make the sign of the cross, pausing as you pray the name of each person.

Ignatius's Words

The spiritual journal of Ignatius is replete with references to the holy Trinity and with visions of and prayers to God, Jesus, and Spirit. At the beginning of Lent, on Wednesday, February 27, 1544, Ignatius wrote:

I got ready in my room, asking Jesus, not in any way for a confirmation, but that He do me His best service in the presence of the Most Holy Trinity, etc., and by the most suitable manner, provided I find myself in His grace.

In this I received some light and strength, and going into the chapel and praying, I felt or rather saw beyond my natural strength the Most Holy Trinity and Jesus, presenting me, or placing me, or simply being the means of union in the midst of the Most Holy Trinity in order that this intellectual vision be communicated to me. With this knowledge and sight, I was deluged with tears and love, directing to Jesus and to the Most Holy Trinity a respectful worship which was more on the side of a reverential love than anything else.

Later, I thought of Jesus doing the same duty in thinking of praying to the Father, thinking and feeling interiorly that He was doing everything with the Father and the Most Holy Trinity. I began Mass with many tears, great devotion and tears continuing all through it. Likewise all of a sudden, I clearly saw the same vision of the Most Holy Trinity as before, with an ever increasing love for His Divine Majesty, and several times losing the power of speech.

—*Spiritual Journal*, 19

Reflection

Plunged as he was into the mystery of the holy Trinity, Ignatius was moved to an adoration unto tears before the majesty of God.

The trinitarian community . . . is formed by the mutual love of the divine persons, each of whom exists only for the others in the complete self-donation and absolute openness that is the nature of divine love. Each person reserves nothing for himself, and everything is given to and received from the others, forming the mystery of mutual love and communion, which is their unity of essence. Through this mutual love not only is everything common among them, but they are, just as each one of them is, the divine life that is by its nature simply One: [as Pedro Arrupe said in *The Trinitarian Inspiration of the Ignatian Charism*,] ". . . there is no more life in the three persons than is found in one of them, since the three exist by a real identity in the same divine being. In them, and only in them, the unity of love is the unity of essence." (*Placed with Jesus*, 378)

This ecstatic outpouring among the three persons of the Trinity was grace and model for Ignatius, both in his love for his community and in his service in the church. This trinitarian love also serves us as a model of our love for God, for each other, and for our service.

▶ Meditate on each of the following questions. If you find writing helpful, jot down your reflections.

- To what actions is the Creator calling me? How can I be a co-creator for the reign of God?
- How am I most effectively "putting on" Jesus Christ? How am I showing God's human face to my sisters and brothers?
- How am I open to the Holy Spirit? Do I call upon the wisdom and fire of the Spirit to help me make decisions and act courageously?
- How am I building communities of love as imaged in the Trinity?

▶ Margaret Clitherow was put to death at York, England, in 1586, during the suppression of Catholicism. In his poem in her honor, Gerard Manley Hopkins invoked the Trinity in a unique and definitive Ignatian way. Read this segment of the poem, and ponder the image of the Trinity portrayed in it:

The Christ-ed beauty of her mind
Her mould of features mated well.
She was a woman, upright, outright;
Her will was bent at God. . . .
She caught the crying of those Three,
The Immortals of the eternal ring,
The Utterer, Utterèd, Uttering,
And witness in her place would she.
—"Margaret Clitherow," in *Poems and Prose*, 78–79

How does your life catch, witness, and mirror the "Utterer, Utterèd, and Uttering"—the Lover, Loved, and Loving that is our tri-une God?

► In honor of the Trinity, be particularly generous toward other people today. Build community in any way you can.

► Pray for peace within you, with other people, and among all humankind.

From God's Word

And Jesus came and said to them, " All authority in heaven and on earth has been given to me. Go therefore and make disciples of all nations, baptizing them in the name of the Father and of the Son and of the Holy Spirit, and teaching them to obey everything that I have commanded you. And remember, I am with you always, to the end of the age."

—Matthew 28:18–20

Closing prayer: Glory be to God, through the Son, in the Holy Spirit.

For Further Reading

Brodrick, James. *Saint Ignatius Loyola: The Pilgrim Years, 1491–1538.* New York: Farrar, Straus and Cudahy, 1956.

Dalmases, Cándido de. *Ignatius of Loyola, Founder of the Jesuits: His Life and Work.* Trans. Jerome Aixalá. St. Louis, MO: Institute of Jesuit Sources, 1985.

Fleming, David L. *The Spiritual Exercises of Saint Ignatius: A Literal Translation and a Contemporary Reading.* St. Louis, MO: Institute of Jesuit Sources, 1978.

Olin, John C., ed., and Joseph F. O'Callaghan, trans. *The Autobiography of Saint Ignatius Loyola.* New York: Harper and Row, 1974.

Purcell, Mary. *The First Jesuit: Saint Ignatius Loyola (1491–1556).* Chicago: Loyola University Press, 1981.

Rahner, Karl. *Ignatius of Loyola.* Trans. Rosaleen Oekenden. London: Collins, 1978.

Tetlow, Elisabeth Meier, trans. *The Spiritual Exercises of Saint Ignatius Loyola.* Lanham, MD: University Press of America, 1987.

Young, William J., ed. and trans. *Letters of Saint Ignatius of Loyola.* Chicago: Loyola University Press, 1959.

Young, William J., trans. *The Spiritual Journal of Saint Ignatius Loyola, February 1544–1545*. Woodstock, MD: Woodstock College Press, 1958.

Acknowledgments

The psalms quoted in this book are from *Psalms Anew*, compiled by Nancy Schreck and Maureen Leach (Winona, MN: Saint Mary's Press, 1986). Copyright © 1986 by Saint Mary's Press. Used with permission. All rights reserved.

Some scriptural material is freely adapted. These adaptations are not to be understood or used as official translations of the Bible. All other scriptural quotations used in this book are from the New Jerusalem Bible. Copyright © 1985 by Darton, Longman & Todd, Ltd., London, and Doubleday, a division of Random House, Inc., New York.

Selections from *The First Jesuit: Saint Ignatius Loyola (1491–1556)*, by Mary Purcell (Chicago: Loyola University Press, 1981). Copyright © 1981 by Mary Purcell.

Selections from *The Autobiography of Saint Ignatius Loyola*, edited by John C. Olin (Bronx, NY: Fordham University Press, 1993). English language translation copyright © 1974 by John C. Olin and Joseph F. O'Callaghan. Used with permission of Fordham University Press.

Selections from *Ignatius of Loyola*, by Karl Rahner (London: Collins, 1978). Copyright © 1978 by Verlag Herder, Freiburg im Breisgau.

Selections from *The New Book of Christian Prayers*, compiled by Tony Castle (New York: Crossroad Publishing Co., 1987). Copyright © 1986 by Tony Castle.

Selections from *Ignatius of Loyola, Founder of the Jesuits*, by Cándido de Dalmases (Anand, India: Gujarat Sahitya Prakash, 1985). Copyright © 1985 by The Institute of Jesuit Sources.

Selections from *Placed with Jesus Bearing His Cross*, by Richard Ward Dunphy (Rome: Typis Pontificiae Universitiatis Gregorianae, 1983).

Selections from *The Spiritual Exercises of Saint Ignatius*, by David L. Fleming (St. Louis, MO: Fusz Memorial, Saint Louis University, 1978). Copyright © 1978 by The Institute of Jesuit Sources.

Selections from *The Spiritual Journal of Saint Ignatius Loyola, February 1544–1545*, translated by William J. Young (Woodstock, MD: Woodstock College Press, 1958). Used with permission.

Selections from "Friends in the Lord," by Javier Osuna, in *The Way* 3 (1974). Copyright © 1974 by James Walsh, SJ.

Selections from *The Divine Milieu*, by Pierre Teilhard de Chardin (New York: Harper Torchbooks, 1960). Copyright © 1957 by Editions du Seuil, Paris. English translation copyright 1960 by William Collins Sons & Co., London, and Harper & Row Publishers, New York. Renewed 1988 by Harper & Row Publishers, Inc.

Selections from "Obedience," in *The Oxford Book of Prayer*, edited by George Appleton (New York: Oxford University Press, 1985). Copyright © 1985 by George Appleton.

University Press, 1959). Copyright © 1959, 1969 by Princeton University Press.

Selections from "Te Deum," in *Hymns to the Church*, by Gertrude von Le Fort, translated by Margaret Chanler (New York: Sheed & Ward, 1953).

The prayer Soul of Christ from *Hearts on Fire: Praying with Jesuits*, edited by Michael Harter, SJ (Chicago: Loyola Press, 1993, 2004).

About the Authors

Jacqueline Bergan and Marie Schwan, CSJ, have ministered separately and together for over 38 years and have not only an astute knowledge of Ignatian spirituality, but a deep love for the Spiritual Exercises. Through their retreats and spiritual direction, Bergan and Schwan have guided men and women, lay and religious through the Exercises. They collaborated on writing several books based on Ignatian spirituality, including the five-volume *Take and Receive* series, based on the Spiritual Exercises of St. Ignatius.

Jacqueline Bergan offers spiritual direction through Sacred Ground Spirituality Center in St. Paul, MN, and Spiritual Directors International. She lives with her husband Leonard and family in Bear Trap Lake, WI.

Marie Schwan, CSJ, was a member of the Congregation of St. Joseph. She spent a number of years focused on post-Vatican II and biblical renewal within her community and beyond, including 14 years as associate director of the Jesuit Retreat House in Oshkosh, WI. Marie Schwan passed away on December 30, 2014.